HERALDRY OF THE OCEANS

HERALDRY OF THE OCEANS
THE GARB OF THE MERCHANT SEAFARER

ALASTAIR ARNOTT

The History Press

First published 2015

The History Press
The Mill, Brimscombe Port
Stroud, Gloucestershire, GL5 2QG
www.thehistorypress.co.uk

British Library Cataloguing in Publication Data.
A catalogue record for this book is available from the British Library.

ISBN 978 0 7524 9341 1

Typesetting and origination by The History Press
Printed in China

CONTENTS

FOREWORD

I am hugely honoured to be asked to write the foreword in a book that covers such an important but, until now, unrecorded part of our maritime heritage. When I joined my first ship as an apprentice with Shaw Savill & Albion (SSA) Line in 1964, the United Kingdom had the largest merchant fleet in the world. The design and name of a ship was often enough to identify its owners and SSA was no exception. What also distinguished a shipping company was the uniform, or at least the braid, buttons and cap badges, worn by its seafarers. The badges in particular were works of art and often, like the one I then wore, encompassed the company's house flag. We may not of have been conscious of it at the time but we wore our uniforms with a sense of pride – we were, after all, part of a great company in the greatest merchant fleet the world had ever known. Even today I still have all my badges and braid spanning my twenty-nine years at sea.

This book includes an astonishing number of badges and uniforms which, in reality, make up a microcosm of this once huge industry, with its wonderful traditions. For people like me the contents evoke memories of great times that are sadly all but vanished in this technologically driven world. Once again Alastair Arnott has added a much needed and hugely welcome piece of work to the annals of our maritime history.

Captain David Parsons, MNM MNI
Chief Executive, Merchant Navy Welfare Board
Southampton

Acknowledgements

The author is extremely grateful to a number of individuals and organisations, an alphabetical list of which follows. Each has made a significant contribution, whether in relation to a single point or whether we stayed in contact over several years.

A few of these must be singled out for specific mention. Both the Honourable Company of Master Mariners at the Embankment in London and Southampton Master Mariners allowed free access to their badge collections in order that the knowledge therein could be recorded. Dorset County Archives very kindly allowed the reproduction of the rare and early photograph of Commander Woolcott. The author's main collaborator from early days has been Commander, now Doctor Terry Lilley. Without their help, encouragement and support this book would not have been possible.

People

Bob Abel
Richard Alexander
Capt. G. Angas
Linda Barton
Capt. Eric Beetham
Alan Bloor
Nigel Bond
Stephen Booth
Mark Bowen
Elise Chainey
Alasdair Chalmers
Adrian Clutterbuck
Diana Coode
Suzie Cox
James Davenport
David Denholm
Shirley Driscoll
Roger Dye
Philip Frost

Ian Gibb
Jim Grant
Charles Haas
Capt. Lionel Hall
David Hamilton
Ron. Hancock
Commander Graham Hockley
Richard James
Sheila Jemima
Dr David Jenkins
Karen Jones
Andrew King
Dr Terry Lilley
Dr Bridget McConnell
Graham Mackenzie
Ian Middleditch
Rachel Mulhearn
Peter Newall
Eleni Papavasilelou

Capt. David Parsons
Capt. Graham Pepper
Commander Tom Peppitt
Barry Powell
Jonathan Quail
Stuart Rankin
Jim Rees
Peter Sara
Ian Stockbridge, MNM
Richard Stokes
Gordon Sykes-Little
Matthew Tanner, MBE
Capt. Barry Thompson
Tony Tibbles
Peter Tilley
Commodore R.W. Warwick
Capt. Michael White
Andrew Wilson
Jackie Winstanley

ORGANISATIONS

ART (GB) Ltd
Beamish the North of England Open Air Museum
Clyde River Steamer Club
Honourable Company of Master Mariners
Corporation of Trinity House
Davis Service Group PLC
Dorset County Council (Dorset History Centre)
Dundee Art Galleries and Museums (Dundee City Council)
Dundee, Perth and London Shipping

Co. Ltd
Earby and District Local History Society
Gieves and Hawkes Ltd
Glasgow Life
G & SWR Association
Marconi Veterans' Association
Merchant Navy Association
Merseyside Maritime Museum
Miller, Rayner Ltd
National Maritime Museum
National Museums of Wales
National Railway Museum

Nautilus
Preston Historical Society
Royal National Lifeboat institution
RN Library, Portsmouth
Scottish Maritime Museum
SELEX Communications Ltd
Southampton City Archives
Southampton Master Mariners Club
SS Great Britain Trust
Toye, Kenning and Spencer Ltd
Tyne and Wear Museum Library
William Scully ltée

INTRODUCTION

This book has been inspired by the collections held in museums that relate to the lives of merchant seafarers, and particularly the uniforms worn by members of the British Merchant Navy. It concentrates primarily on the designation markings and badges of these companies rather than the cut of the garments themselves.

Those researching this subject, particularly those with an interest in family history, often want to know about their relatives or individuals who have played a part in the lives of people that were important to them. Generally it is known that the person in question had been in the Merchant Service at some time, but what is not often known was with what company he or she had worked or in what capacity. In many cases a photograph of the individual concerned or a scrap of embroidered cloth might survive as a clue to employment or occupation but it isn't always easy to find the right source to be able to identify the significance of small elements of uniform or insignia. This sort of detail is of vital importance to family researchers, although accurate information on the subject has proved hard to find. Furthermore, in the period from about the 1970s onward, the maritime strength of the country and the number of companies associated with the sea has diminished to a very great extent.

The greatest sadness is that those with the knowledge and understanding of Merchant Navy uniforms are now becoming fewer in number. Worse still, even those employed in later years and who are fit and able do not always have a clear recollection of the details. For example, oral testimony from a man who had been a steward with one of the cross-Channel ferry companies revealed that, for a time, this steward had to wear a different tie travelling in each direction: a blue one going one way and a red one for the other. By the time the story was being told this individual could no longer remember which was which: did a red tie mean he was going to or coming from France? Likewise a nursing sister who had changed companies during her career had not noticed until it was pointed out to her that the rank markings on her shoulder straps changed orientation. With the Royal Mail Line the straps were of red cloth over gold braid and with the Pacific Steam Navigation Company they were made of gold braid over red cloth, both designating the same role and rank.

The single factor that led directly to the writing of this book was a request for a detailed description of the cap badge of ships' officers employed by the Great Eastern Railway during the First World War. This was from individuals in Belgium who were planning a commemorative service to mark the ninetieth anniversary of the execution of Captain Fryatt and it turned out that they had already approached the National Railway Museum and the history society dealing with matters relating to the Great Eastern Railway. Neither organisation had been able to come up with an answer to what seemed to be quite a straightforward request. If this sort of information had been lost after such a relatively short interval of time, what else had been lost, or more productively, what was in danger of following the same route? The matter was particularly pressing because of the rapid changes that had taken place in the merchant fleet and its rapid decline in size and stature as the twentieth century progressed.

So, one way of using this book would be to try to identify the badge or shipping line insignia worn by the person being researched. Buttons tend to be a little small and indistinct in photographs and have therefore not been included here. The next step might be to look for appropriate rank markings and their meaning, which of course changed over time and differed from company to company. Of course it must be remembered that the smaller shipping companies had no uniform of any kind other than perhaps a company cap badge. In these circumstances employees requiring new clothing would in all likelihood have purchased off-the-peg generic items from a local supplier.

It may be that a group of medals exists or is visible in a photograph, in which case some inferences might be drawn about the person's activities and an approximate date ascribed to the image. It is not, of course, always possible to see details of medal ribbons, especially if the photograph is black and white or sepia, but it is often possible to narrow down the possibilities by checking against dates of birth or medal records where they have survived.

For those who want to know more about the background to the industries of gold wire and badge manufacture some information has been included here. There is also some information relating to the industries concerned with the manufacture and supply of specialist garments connected with seafaring activity. These secondary trades were very extensive at one time and provided employment for significant numbers of people with no other links to the sea.

Some lore associated with dress among our merchant seafarers is also examined and myths debunked. In the absence of definitive records, some assessment has also been made of the number of types of badge that may at one time have existed and of which little or no trace remains today.

1

GOLD WIRE MANUFACTURE

People have always been fascinated by gold. It does not tarnish under normal circumstances and retains its bright metallic appearance indefinitely. It can be rolled, beaten and twisted into shape and very small quantities can be made into wire or thread and used in the weaving of, or decoration applied to, cloth.

It is only natural therefore that gold in various forms has been used for ornament and incorporated into garments for millennia, conveying an impression of rank and status both by virtue of its appearance and implied by the cost of such a precious metal.

The processes used to produce gold in a form that was both relatively economical in use while enhancing its reflective properties have remained pretty much unchanged for the last 200 years until the present day.

Both gold wire and gold thread are used in the production of garments and their various parts, as described in the following chapters. Gold thread has a fibre core such as cotton or silk with a very thin layer of gold foil wound round its exterior, gold being conveniently the most malleable and ductile of metals. Nowadays artificial fibre for the core material is also an option, which in many cases has the advantage of being less susceptible to damp and other causes of rot. Gold wire, on the other hand, is solid although it does not consist of gold throughout, but has a very thin layer of gold over a substrate of silver alloy or silver and copper.

The conventional way of making gold wire was to start with a large billet as shown in the illustration on p. 25 and to draw this out in successive stages to produce thinner and thinner wire. After each drawing operation the wire produced is annealed, that is, heated sufficiently to regain its original softness. By this method the ratio of gold to the other metals remains constant.

As gold and silver are assayable, careful control is kept of the proportion of gold used in relation to the other metals so that the ratio of one to the other meets the required standard. It is sometimes the case that 'silver'

wire is used in badge manufacture and this can be produced by exactly the same method without the gold exterior layer. Cheaper grades of gold wire can be produced by means of electroplating a layer of gold onto the core. The better grades of wire, on the other hand, have gold leaf burnished onto the exterior of the core before the process of drawing out begins.

Wire as described above is not used directly for badge manufacture, but undergoes further work to enhance its reflective properties and to give it greater apparent bulk. There are several popular forms for the wire used in badge production where the wire is twisted round a former. This is simply a length of wire or rod, made with a predetermined cross-section and in a range of sizes. The gold wire is wound round the former to make a tight spiral which, when slipped off the former, can make the wire look different and more exciting. In the case of 'pearl purl' for example, a former that is circular in cross section is used to give the finished wire the appearance of a string of golden pearls. 'Lizarine' is a variant of this in which the manufacturing process flattens the exterior face of the wire giving a more tubular appearance.

The other form chiefly encountered is plate. Here the wire is passed through rollers to form a flat strip. This can either be held down at the edges in badge manufacture or more often given a convex form with padding and stitching across the piece which is folded to conceal the stitches as shown on p. 25. There are of course other types of gold wire as a raw material used in the manufacture of dress. One need only look at the loose spring-like coils forming the fringe of naval epaulettes, for example, to find a relatively common and easily recognisable use of the product to create a visual effect. These wires, coming in a wide variety of types, sizes and textures (because the surface can be either lustrous or matt) allow an element of variation in design. David Gieve mentions the use of 'cheeks' in connection with his firm in his book *Gieves and Hawkes 1785–1985*. To make the cheek, gold wire is wound onto a triangular rather than a circular mandrel of needle size, in order to produce a coil with 'corners'. Gold wire used in this way has, however, not been encountered in connection with badges in the Merchant Service.

The actual construction of the badge involves many other processes and materials. To date, no machine has been developed that is capable of working with any of the various forms of gold wire to produce the traditional type of cap badge. The absolute necessity for these embroidered badges to be produced by hand probably accounts in part for why they are so highly prized as distinguishing emblems. The specialised industry concerned with the drawing of gold wire was concentrated in London in the eighteenth century, with Benton and Johnson being one of the last firms concerned with the trade and which became part of the Stephen Simpson empire only in the 1960s. From the middle of the nineteenth century, however, the centre of gold wire production moved to Preston in Lancashire. The firms established in the town included John Sharp from 1850 to 1961 when the firm was taken over by Stephen Simpson; G.H.L. Tootell from 1861 to 1908; E. & W.G. Makinson Ltd which was wound up in 1926; and Stephen Simpson which lasted from 1862 until 1991.

Incidentally, the reason for the concentration of manufacture in Preston was its proximity to the seat of cotton cloth manufacture. Because cotton cloth was bleached after weaving, the weavers had to identify themselves as producers of a given length of cotton by marking the finished fabric using metallic thread. This was because distinguishing marks made of coloured cotton would have been bleached out, and therefore invisible, after processing. It was important for the individual that the markings should remain in order that they could be paid for their work, and so a local metallic wire industry grew up close to the cotton mills.

Gold Wire Badge Manufacture

A typical manufacturer of badges would have a design department to which the shipping company would address its initial requirements. From this an agreed finished design would emerge in the form of an outline drawing. This drawing, on tracing paper and actual size, would then be used to create a stencil. In the case of one of the former leading manufacturers, Stephen Simpson, the stencil was made from a thin brass sheet. A needle was pushed through the tracing paper, following the pattern, to leave a pattern of little holes in the brass and so transferring the design to the metal. A part number was also marked onto the stencil by the same method and at the same time so it could be identified later.

The embroideress (the operatives were usually women) was supplied with the stencil and a card bearing the same picture of the finished design. She was also given instructions regarding the final appearance of the finished badge and, more often than not, samples of the wires to be used.

The brass stencil was placed over black felt and French chalk paste applied by means of a stencil brush to transfer the design cleanly to the fabric. The outline of the badge was then cut out. Black cotton fabric was tensioned in a wooden frame of sufficient size for four to six of the prepared felt shapes to be stuck to the tensioned backing cloth with a mould-resistant adhesive.

The embroideress, seated on a cast iron stool, set to work on all the badges held on the frame at the same time, aided by the instruction card and surrounded by the materials needed to do the job. The frame on which she worked was held firmly and at an angle by two iron bars. A badge of average size and complexity took a skilled worker between three and four hours to complete each one. The badge was finished by being cut from the frame and by having a stiff backing pasted and ironed on. Finished badges were placed in a box for inspection by the embroidery room manager and only if the work was up to standard would the woman who produced the badges get paid the appropriate piecework rate.

A hand embroidery department was established in Stephen Simpson's factory in 1898. Although there were a significant number of embroideresses employed on site, the firm also employed outworkers. These were often skilled workers who had left to start a family and although still retaining the necessary skills to do the job might also have appreciated the relative freedom to fit the work round domestic activities. In its heyday in the 1930s there were ninety women employed in the embroidery department and a further thirty outworkers who produced badges at home.

The method of working described above is shown for an Indian Air Force cap badge, produced by Stephen Simpson, in the illustrations on p. 26. Other manufacturers used slightly different techniques. A cardboard template from an as-yet-unidentified manufacturer, this time a modern Cunard cap badge, is also shown on p. 26. Sufficient instructions were given on the card to enable the design to be executed when transferred to the fabric. We learn that 'best port cloth' was to be used, that the lion was metal and that the crown was to be embroidered 'as drawn'. Various other instructions are given about the leaves, stems and berries. Two of the most significant facts to be found written on this card are that the design was to executed in 'gold when for Glasgow' and 'best gilt when for Liverpool', and the number of the design: 104,453. Why there was a difference in

1914

1918

quality of the finished badges supplied against orders from the different ports is not known. It may have depended on the relative standing of the tailoring firm being supplied, in which case the ultimate customer, the seafarer, would be unaware of any difference unless he was able to compare the retail cost of the finished product. That cost, incidentally, is not recorded in the archives of the badge or clothing manufacturer. The large number suggests that a great range of designs must have been produced in this fashion, although there were many trades and professions requiring badges and insignia other than seafarers.

It is unfortunate that no record seems to have survived from any manufacturer listing the shipping companies for which badges were produced as this would be very helpful to researchers and collectors alike. Many written records have been lost owing to changes of ownership: the Cunard card mentioned above was a chance retrieval from a skip, and the Stephen Simpson templates were sent for recycling when the firm closed because, being brass, they had a high scrap value. The Lancashire County Record Office has a small quantity of general records from Stephen Simpson's works which were retrieved in 2009. All early Gieves records were lost as a result of the bombing of the Bond Street premises in September 1940 and both the Liverpool and Southampton offices that specialised in Merchant Naval work were themselves destroyed by enemy action during the Second World War.

An enquiry sent to Gieves seeking information on the merchant shipping companies to which badges were supplied elicited the true but unhelpful response that they made badges for 'most of them'. Cap badges from Gieves that had features such as an imperial crown were more expensive than those sourced elsewhere but were distinguished from those of other suppliers by being padded to give a three-dimensional shape which was highly prized. This solid, three-dimensional look can be seen in the oblique view of a Gieves and Hawkes badge on p. 45.

By the beginning of the twenty-first century much of the business of manufacturing badges had moved overseas, particularly to Pakistan and India. Some of the best cap badges being produced today are made by the family firm of Widelinks Inc., which has been in operation for over sixty years and is based in Varanasi. Formerly known as Benares, the city is perhaps best known for its long tradition of producing decorative and ornamental metalwork and therefore has a workforce with the necessary skills to work with wire and thread. Widelinks Inc. have another method of maintaining consistency of quality and appearance of the finished product. Rather than using a perforated brass template to store the design whenever a new badge is commissioned, an extra badge is made and stored for reference. This is the case even if the order is for only one badge. If ever a repeat order is received, the prototype can be retrieved and copied using traditional hand methods. In the West we tend to worry about the potential exploitation of young people in this sort of industry. In fact, in this case, nothing could be further from the truth, as India – a fast-developing nation – has high educational standards and its young people are drawn to jobs in high-tech industries. The firm therefore has an ageing workforce and is said to find it hard to recruit younger trainees.

Another important element of uniform is gold distinction lace, the technical description for the gold braid used, for example, around the cuffs of sleeves to denote rank. The manufacture of lace was often undertaken by specialist lacemen, obtaining their gold thread and wire from firms like Stephen Simpson. One of the best known lacemen was David Kenning of Coventry, a firm that was later taken over by Toye, so that for a time Coventry became the centre of this industry. Joseph Starkey Ltd, a firm that had started in the lace industry in 1835, produced its work on hand looms until at least the time when it was taken over by Gieves. The firm of Stephen Simpson itself ventured into lace manufacture on hand looms in Preston in 1855 and introduced power looms into this field only in 1878. The weft, or threads that run across the length of the lace, can be of gold or silver wire, or gold or silver thread, in which case it is known as 'orris' lace.

Joseph Starkey were also gold wire embroiderers, that is badge makers, as were Lawton's of Preston and George H. Fenner in London. All three firms also made gold lace. William Scully Ltee of Montreal, Canada, a firm that was established in 1877, still advertises as being a 'Manufacturer of Merchant Navy braid, hand embroidered and Bullion badges, MN caps including master'. The company has tried other manufacturing techniques and its recent cast bronze cap badge for the Canadian Marine (Navy) is an excellent example. Other badge manufacturers recorded in Britain were Harvey's and A. Oliver & Son of London; Edwards & Co. of Swansea; and Charles Bell & Son of Liverpool, but it is possible that all these firms were simply suppliers who rebranded with their own names the goods that were made elsewhere.

When the firm of Stephen Simpson (Northern Counties) Ltd had a brief revival after its collapse in 1991 the hand and machine embroidery sections, which had diminished greatly in size by that time, were taken over by Toye, Kenning and Spencer. The business continued under this ownership until 2009 when the residual business changed yet again to

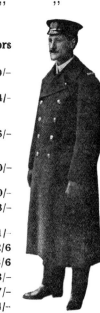
1918

be carried on as DMC Regalia, run by a nucleus of former employees. The new business was heralded by a headline in the local paper which proclaimed 'Titanic Sails Again!', which may, on the face of it, seem a peculiar choice of words. However, there is a popular local legend, accepted as incontrovertible fact, that Simpson's made the uniforms for the crew of the ill-fated liner RMS *Titanic*. Sometimes this story is modified to suggest that it was the regalia of the band that was supplied although one might have expected that musicians performing in an orchestra would wear evening dress. The ornamental cloth 'falls' on the backs of the music stands might though have been produced by Simpson's. In any case there is probably more than a grain of truth in the connection – seamen would have worn tallies on their hats and at the time these would perhaps have been the only items identified as relating to RMS *Titanic* (see Tallies p. 66). Simpson's machine embroidery department could easily have supplied these even if they were only one of a number of suppliers.

It is more difficult to prove a connection between Simpson's and the 'family' of White Star Line cap badges (see badge nos 292 to 295 on p. 45 for illustrations) as none of these are ship-specific and crew often switched within vessels of the company fleet. Captain Smith himself was transferred at short notice from the *Olympic* to the *Titanic*. We cannot be certain, but it is more than likely that a proportion of this embroidery work was supplied by Simpson's to the various tailoring firms of the day. It is also likely that a number of the buttons worn by crew of any rank were also pressed by Simpson's as the company had a button making department that was active until 1930.

Another widely told story relates to Simpson's clandestine efforts during the Second World War and shows that even the activities of this industry could be far from humdrum. The son of the Managing Director of Simpson's, who was still employed by the firm in the 1960s, tells the story that he once found, stuffed at the back of a desk drawer, a felt panel with badges used by the German Luftwaffe during the Second World War. A quiet conversation with his father revealed that the firm had maintained a select group of embroideresses who were obliged to sign the Official Secrets Act. These women were housed in a separate workshop away from their colleagues and apart from being allowed out for breaks and to use the toilet were effectively kept shut away. The reason for this high level of secrecy was that the women were engaged in the production of accurate replica German air force insignia for use in secret activities, including espionage. In order to be authentic, the correct aluminium wire, as used on Luftwaffe uniforms, was obtained at high personal risk by members of the Dutch resistance and eventually found its way to the Simpson's factory. The finished badges were supplied to the War Office for use. This project, it is said, was undertaken in early 1944. Aluminium has different reflective properties from silver and would develop a grey appearance rather than remaining shiny like the usual Simpson materials, although it is not recorded if aluminium wire handled differently when being made up. Whatever the difficulties encountered by these women in the production of the replica insignia, the difference in appearance of British and German metal wire made it of vital importance that the correct materials were used if the clandestine operations were to have any chance of success.

2

MANUFACTURE OF BADGES AND LACE

The finished garment produced by a tailor is an assemblage of components that themselves have been sourced from a range of suppliers, so the fabric, lining and thread, for example, will all have come from different manufacturers. The elements that concern us and that primarily differentiate one shipping company and one rank from another are the badges, buttons and lace.

Buttons, though similar to each other in size, form and colour, are as pictorially variable as cap badges and have not been considered to any extent here except to note some of the principal suppliers and to use the appropriate button in an illustration where necessary. There are reference works covering the subject such as *Buttons: A Guide for Collectors* by Gwen Squire for example, but other sources of information are available. The patterns for buttons for Merchant Navy 'standard' uniform and their uses were stipulated at the time of its creation, but followed existing conventions (see the second page of George Kenning's catalogue, p. 23).

Nearly all the cap badges considered here are handmade and have various types of metallic 'gold' or occasionally 'silver' thread as the principal constituent. A very few specimens are metal pressings which, when new, are a very accurate representation of the close stitching of gold leaves. These should not be confused with the use of pressed or enamelled metal elements that are often incorporated in individual badges. Company emblems or house flags often consist of an enamel insertion because they do not embroider easily on such a small scale, and naval crowns and anchors of various forms are similarly applied as separate pieces.

In very recent times, computer-controlled embroidering machines have been able to copy the intricate pattern of traditional cap badges but as yet cannot handle metallic wires, nor can they achieve the solidity of the handmade product which continues to be widely used. The Honourable Company of Master Mariners does have an example of what appears to be a machine-stitched badge in its Algoma Central Marine cap badge.

Uniform
of all kinds

Everyone admires uniform—chiefly because of its neatness and undoubted smartness when it is properly cut and made. Only experienced uniform tailors can give the fit and neatness requisite in any kind of formal dress, and stewardesses who like to feel that their uniform is of irreproachable cut and fit, made from the very finest materials and possessing the distinctive superiority of real quality are those whose outfits have been supplied by us.

We are official outfitters to most of the great shipping lines and the manageresses at the branches below are thoroughly conversant with stewardesses' needs and know the exact regulation styles of all the companies. All White Star requirements (women's department) are stocked and urgent special orders can be completed in a few hours.

The laundry-proof Apron illustrated here is a specimen of the quality of our work. It was specially designed for sea-going stewardesses, and is made from linen-finished cloth which resists laundering and hard wear to a remarkable degree. Call and see one at

Nurses' Outfitting
Association, Ltd.,
57b, Renshaw Street
LIVERPOOL.
LONDON : 179, Victoria Street, S.W.1.
SOUTHAMPTON : 3, Above Bar (1st Floor).

1927

Perhaps in these cost-conscious times, the perfection and easy reproducibility of machine-stitching may be the way forward. The production of cap badges for the Merchant Service continues to be a laborious handcraft process and sadly one which appears not to be practised any longer in Britain.

The simplest study of cap badges will reveal that, with several potential manufacturers and much scope for interpretation along the line, each individual badge is unique. No two are ever quite identical in spite of the intention to provide a 'brand' or identity for the company concerned, and this is the great charm of an object that is produced with good quality materials and by a skilled hand.

If only a few records have survived the question arises of how we are to get a reliable picture of what was made and for which companies? Company regulations, while they might appear to be a useful source, have their limitations. For example, only the post-Second World War book of regulations of the British India Steam Navigation Company carries useful illustrations and in fact almost none carry any illustrations at all, relying on a written description, or, with the earliest examples, leaving a lot to chance and a collective understanding of what was 'right'. The earliest Royal Mail Steam Packet Co. regulations, for example, state that, in respect of the badge, 'an example can be seen at head office'.

Unfortunately that note was written over 160 years ago and is profoundly unhelpful in connection with current research. In addition, written descriptions can and do appear to be faulty as with the 1927 Cunard regulations which clearly state that the Cunard lion, when used for the badges of 'Inspectors, Storekeepers and Chief Stewards, etc.', was to be placed in a lozenge. Now a 'lozenge' has a specific meaning in heraldic terms and indicates the use of a diamond shape, although real examples of badges recorded in historic collections have all been in the form of an ellipse, or oval, as shown in the drawings on p. 29. We do not really know what was intended, so perhaps the manufacturer produced what was felt to be most appropriate or visually pleasing.

The use of a diamond as an element of badge design is not very common and the Honourable Company of Master Mariners has only one example of a cap badge from a foreign company in this form. Otherwise only a few company house flags, translated into badges, include a diamond. Examples include Chadwick, Wainwright & Co., M. Moss & Co. and of course Alfred Holt. Evidently, we can refer only to those examples that have actually survived to get as true a picture as possible, or as a second best option, examine photographs. Some illustrations in the form of drawings do still exist, although they are not necessarily correct and must be treated with caution by the researcher.

3

Examples of Company Cap Badges

This book reproduces nearly 300 drawings of cap badges which it is hoped are representative of the industry. They include examples from 230 shipping companies although training institutions and the 'standard' Merchant Navy badges, which could be worn by any appropriately qualified person from any shipping company, are also included. In the larger companies that used their own identifying badge there is often a hierarchy of types depending on rank. Examples of these 'families' of badges are given.

The badges themselves:

1. Aberdeen Line: George Thompson & Co.: an early badge (compare with nos 2 and 257).
2. Aberdeen & Commonwealth: formed by the joining of 1 and 21.
3. Albyn Line: Allan, Black & Co.
4. Alcoa Shipping.
5. Alexandra Towing Co.: Howard Smith (UK) Ltd, from 1993.
6. Algoma Central Marine: a machine-stitched version, non-metallic thread.
7. Anchor Brocklebank Line: T. & J. Brocklebank Ltd: one of the few badge designs with a black wreath.
8. Anchor Line: Henderson Brothers.
9. Andrew Weir Shipping & Trading Co. Ltd: with naval crown in pressed metal.
10. Anglo-American Telegraph Co.: Henry Weaver.
11. Anglo Saxon Petroleum Co. Ltd: with enamel flag.
12. Anglo Saxon Petroleum Co. Ltd: the company also operated vessels for Shell Co. of East Africa and Shell Co. (Malta) Ltd with oak leaves.
13. ARC Marine.
14. Asiatic SN Co.: Turner & Co.
15. Associated British Ports.
16. Associated Container Transportation.
17. Associated Steamships.
18. Athel Line: United Molasses Co. Ltd: enamel house flag.
19. Atlantic SN Co.
20. Atlantic Transport Co.
21. Australian Commonwealth Government Line of Steamers: with enamel flag. Became Aberdeen & Commonwealth Line in 1928.
22. Australind Steam Shipping: Trinder, Anderson & Co.: with enamel flag.
23. Bank Line: Weir & Co.
24. Bedouin SN Co.: W. & R. Thomson.
25. Belfast Steamship Co.: part of Coast Lines from about 1940: oak wreath with shield depicting arms of Belfast.
26. Bell Line: James Bell & Co.
27. Ben Line: William Thomson & Co.
28. Bibby Line: Bibby Brothers & Co.: early design.
29. Bibby Line.
30. Bibby Line: with embroidered naval crown.
31. J.A. Billmier & Co. Ltd: naval crown in pressed metal.
32. Blue Star Line: later Blue Star Line (1920) Ltd: part of Vestey Group which bought Booth Line and Lamport & Holt in 1946 (see nos 37 and 160).
33. M.H. Bland & Co.
34. Blandford Shipping: an example of 'Bombay rose' where the crown is an affectation.
35. Blandford Shipping: both this and the previous example have enamel house flags.

36. Booker Line Ltd: note the crown here is a female one (Queen Elizabeth II).
37. Booth Line: A. Booth & Co. (associated company, Booth Iquitos SS Co. Ltd).
38. C.T. Bowring.
39. British & African SN Co.: taken over by Elder, Dempster & Co. in 1889.
40. British Antarctic Survey: example of a royal crown, in this case female, and oak wreath.
41. British Channel Islands Shipping Co.
42. British Channel Island Ferries.
43. Normandy Ferries.
44. British & Commonwealth, also later used by subsidiaries such as Clan Line (no. 72): with no. 45, examples where absence of a crown denotes a Petty Officer.
45. British & Commonwealth Petty Officer: the sea lion is very similar to no. 66.
46. British Columbia Ferries: with enamel shield and female crown.
47. British India SN Co.
48. British & Irish SP Co.: became part of the extensive Coast Lines Seaway (see no. 74).
49. BP Tanker Co.
50. British Ministry of War Transport: First World War design with khaki background.
51. British Phosphate Commission.
52. British Rail Seaspeed: with oak wreath and embroidered naval crown.
53. British Tanker Co.: a late example of 'plate' used to bind the laurel leaves.
54. British Transport Docks Board: an entirely metal design favoured by dock companies for deck hands and shoreside workers. Officers wore the bollard symbol in a circle surrounded by a gold wreath.
55. Bullard King & Co., Natal Line.
56. Burmah Oil Co.: became Burmah-Castrol in 1966 and was acquired by BP in 2000.
57. Burns & Laird: also later part of the Coast Lines group.
58. Burries Markes.
59. Cairn Line of Steamships Ltd, Cairns, Young & Noble.
60. Caledonian Macbrayne.
61. Caledonian Steam Packet Co.: in the guise shown here, it was the shipping arm of the Caledonian Railway. For later design, see no. 60.
62. Canadian Australasian Line: enamel flag.
63. Canadian Coastguard: a maple leaf design.
64. CN Marine: with female crown.
65. Canadian National Railways: with female crown.
66. Canadian National Steamships: example of a male royal crown.
67. CP Ships.
68. Canadian Pacific Steamships: like nos 44 and 45, this forms a family or suit of badges with no. 69. CP Ocean Services had the letters 'POS' on the flag surrounded by an elongated 'C', all in blue.
69. Canadian Pacific Steamships Petty Officer.
70. Canadian SS Lines: with enamel flag.
71. China Navigation Co. Ltd: later owned by J. Swire & Sons Ltd.
72. Clan Line: formed British & Commonwealth Line with Union-Castle in 1955.
73. Clan Line: lion on velvet in ellipse by alternative maker to no. 72 above.
74. Coast Lines Ltd: an extensive group that also comprised B & I, Belfast SS Co., Burns & Laird, Aberdeen SN Co., British Channel Islands Shipping and others.
75. Common Brothers: with enamel flag.
76. Commonwealth Sugar Refiners.
77. Wm Cory & Son Ltd: operated ships for British Electricity Authority, later Central Electricity Generating Board, and Associated Portland Cement.
78. Crescent Shipping.
79. Cunard: with pressed metal lion symbol and female crown.
80. Cunard Petty Officer: with male 'imperial' crown: the lion and globe symbol changed slightly with time.
81. Cunard: Stewards, Barkeepers, etc.
82. Cunard: in gold, second- and third-class Chief Stewards, Storekeeper, etc.
83. Cunard: in silver, Inspector.
84. Cunard/White Star Petty Officer: one of a family of cap badges used by the merged companies between 1934 and 1948.
85. J. & T. Brocklebank.
86. Currie Line.
87. Davies & Newman.
88. J. & J. Denholm.
89. Devitt & Moore: with oak wreath.
90. Dominion Line.

91. Dundee, Perth & London.
92. Eagle Oil & Shipping.
93. East African National Shipping.
94. East African Railways & Harbours.
95. Eastern Telegraph Co.
96. Elder Dempster.
97. Elder Dempster.
98. Elders & Fyffes.
99. Elders & Fyffes Petty Officer.
100. Ellerman & Bucknall.
101. Ellerman City Line.
102. Ellerman's Hall Line.
103. Ellerman's Wilson Line: see no. 297 for the original Wilson Line design.
104. F.T. Everard.
105. Federal SN Co.: post-1900.
106. Federal SN Co.: early design.
107. James Fisher.
108. Furness/Prince Line.
109. Furness Withy & Co.
110. Furness Withy & Co.
111. Furness Withy.
112. Furness Withy Shipping: a modern badge designed by competition c. 1980.
113. J. & G. Gardiner.
114. GPO Cable Ships.
115. GPO Cable Ships Petty Officer.
116. General SN Co.
117. General SN Co.
118. Gilbert & Ellis Islands Marine.
119. Great Eastern Railway.
120. Glasgow Corporation.
121. Glasgow & South Western Railway.
122. Glen Line.
123. Glen Line.
124. Glen Line.
125. Arthur Guinness.
126. HM Coast Guard: see also Gieves' padded version, no. 298.
127. HM Customs: pressed metal version used during the Second World War.
128. HMS *Conway*: also seen with navy blue velvet background.
129. HMS *Worcester*.
130. T. & J. Harrison.
131. Henderson Line.
132. Henderson Line.
133. Holm Line.
134. A. Holt.
135. A. Holt.
136. A. Holt/Glen Line.
137. Hong Kong Islands SS Co.
138. Houlder Bros.
139. Houlder Bros.
140. R.P. Houston.
141. Hoverlloyd.
142. Hoverspeed.
143. Hudson SS Co.
144. Hudson's Bay Co.
145. Hull Gates Shipping.
146. Hull Trinity House.
147. Hunting & Son.
148. Indo China SN Co.
149. International Maritime Carriers.
150. Irish Shipping.
151. Isle of Man SP Co.
152. Isle of Man SP Co.
153. Isle of Man SP Co.
154. Isle of Man SP Co.
155. Jamaica Direct Fruit Line Petty Officer.
156. Kelly Shipping.
157. Kiripati Marine.
158. Lambert Bros.
159. Lambert Bros.
160. Lamport & Holt.
161. Larinaga Steamship Co.
162. Lawther Lata.
163. Leyland Line: the original design was almost identical to no. 27, replaced with this in early 1920s.
164. Liverpool & N. Wales SS Co.: the house flag was embroidered on guernseys of ratings.
165. London Nautical College.

166. Port of London Authority Petty Officer.
167. London & South Western Railway.
168. Lobitos Oilfields.
169. David MacBrayne: see also Caledonian MacBrayne, no. 60.
170. Manchester Liners.
171. Manchester Ship Canal Co.
172. Manx Line.
173. Manx Line.
174. Marconi: later replaced with MN Standard badge.
175. McIlwraith & McEacharn.
176. MN College Greenhythe.
177. MN Standard.
178. MN Standard Petty Officer.
179. MN Standard (Bombay).
180. Mercury Shipping.
181. Mersey Docks.
182. R.W. Miller & Co.
183. Mobil Shipping.
184. Mogul Line.
195. M. Moss & Co.
186. Moss Hutchison.
187. Moss SS Co.
188. Nautilus SS Co.
189. Nelson Line.
190. NZ Dept of Railways.
191. NZ Shipping Co.: a composite design with a metal flag in the centre.
192. NZ Shipping/Federal.
193. Nigerian Black Star.
194. North of Scotland, Orkney & Shetland Steamship Co.
195. North Sea Ferries.
196. Commissioners of Northern Lights.
197. Northern SS Co.
198. James Nourse.
199. Ocean Cruise Line.
200. Ocean Fleets.
201. Orient Line: this and no. 202 are examples of where the crown changed, with the passing of King George VI and the accession of Queen Elizabeth II.
202. Orient Line.

203. Orient Line Chief Steward: with silver leaves. The blue-leaved Petty Officer's badge had an enamel house flag.
204. Overseas Containers Ltd: also found with black flag.
205. Pacific SN Co.
206. Palm Line.
207. Palm Line Petty Officer.
208. Panocean.
209. Pardoe & Williams.
210. P&O: sun with face motif began to be replaced by a plain sun from 1947.
211. P&O: now conjoined with the sun, there was still variation in the inclination of the anchor.
212. P&O Petty Officer.
213. P&O: the designer of the revised P&O series of badges based on the company house flag was H. Spanton in 1972.
214. P&O Chief Petty Officer: see also note about Ambassadresses in the text.
215. P&O Petty Officer.
216. Peninsular Searoad.
217. Port Line: has remained the same design since Tyser Line days. Originally fabric badge rather than enamel. This particular one has a crown: see 'Bombay roses' above.
218. Port Line: a metal badge.
219. Portsmouth Harbour Ferry Co.
220. Prince Line.
221. Reardon Smith.
222. Reardon Smith Nautical College.
223. Red Funnel.
224. Red Funnel Petty Officer.
225. Ropner Shipping.
226. Royal Army Service Corps.
227. Royal Fleet Auxiliary (large).
228. Royal Fleet Auxiliary (small)
229. Royal Maritime Auxiliary Service.
230. RMS *Wray Castle*: in Ambleside, Cumbria, The Radio Officers' Training College.
231. Royal National Lifeboat Institution Coxswain: RNLI became 'Royal' in 1898. During the 1920s, the lettering on badge was RNL-BI.
232. RNLI: Crew.
233. RNLI: Mechanic.

234. Royal Mail Line.
235. Royal Mail Line.
236. Royal Mail SP Co.: some early examples seem to have a wooden flagstaff.
237. Royal Mail Line Petty Officer: also used for deck and engine room ratings and in silver for catering department ratings.
238. Royal Mail/PSN Co.: from the short-lived joint services of the early 1920s.
239. Royal Mail/PSN Co. Petty Officer.
240. Royal Navy Reserve: the RNR was formed in 1859 and like the RN, originally had a Civil and a Military branch. The badge of the Civil Branch was all gold and that of the Military Branch had a silver anchor under the crown and a scalloped top edge of the crown. The letters were gold in both cases. Later both branches merged and used the silver and gold badge. This was also the badge of Pangbourne Nautical College.
241. RN Transport.
242. C. Rowbotham & Son.
243. Walter Runciman.
244. Sail Training Association.
245. Safmarine: successors to Union-Castle nos 282 and 283.
246. Saguenay Shipping
247. Christian Salvesen: this badge also seems to have been used by other companies in the group such as the South Georgia Co. Ltd.
248. Scottish Ship Management.
249. Sealink Newhaven: the flag is that of the original company, the London Brighton & South Coast Railway.
250. Sealink British Ferries: also the badge worn by employees of Stena Sealink, the device shown forming the top row of lace on the sleeve.
251. Sealion.
252. Seaspeed Purserette: post-1970.
253. Seaspeed Purserette: up to 1970.
254. Sheaf S. Shipping Co.
255. Shaw Savill & Co.
256. Shaw Savill & Albion
257. Shaw Savill/Aberdeen & Commonwealth Petty Officer.
258. Silver Line.
259. Solent Aggregates bearing the funnel rather than the house flag.
260. South African Transport Service.

261. South American Saint.
262. Southern Railway.
263. Southampton Pilots: in the 1920s, Trinity House operated the Pilot Service in London, Southampton and a few other important ports.
264. Stag Line.
265. Strick Line.
266. Sugar Line.
267. Thompson S. Shipping.
268. Thoresen Viking Ferries.
269. Townsend Thoresen Ferries.
270. TS *Mercury*: design based on Royal Naval Chaplain's.
271. Trinder Anderson.
272. Trident Tankers.
273. Trinity House Cutter.
274. Trinity House Elder Brother.
275. Trinity House Elder Brother (pre-1900).
276. Trinity House Officer.
277. Trinity House Petty Officer.
278. Trinity House: possibly an early version of Petty Officer badge.
279. Turnbull Scott.
280. Unicorn Line.
281. Union Line: prior to merger with Castle in 1900, see below.
282. Union-Castle.
283. Union-Castle Petty Officer.
284. Union SS Co. of NZ.
285. United Africa Co.
286. United Baltic Cpn.
287. Upper Lakes Group.
288. Warsash School of Navigation.
289. Watts, Watts & Co.
290. West Hartlepool SN Co.
291. Westcott & Laurence.
292. White Star Line.
293. White Star Line Petty Officer.
294. White Star Line Steward.
295. White Star Line Porter. Also used for other ratings.
296. Wilson Line.
297. Yeoward Brothers.
298. Coast Guard: a superior padded and embroidered badge, compare with no. 126.

MERCHANT NAVY BADGES.

BADGES AND BUTTONS, MERCANTILE MARINES.

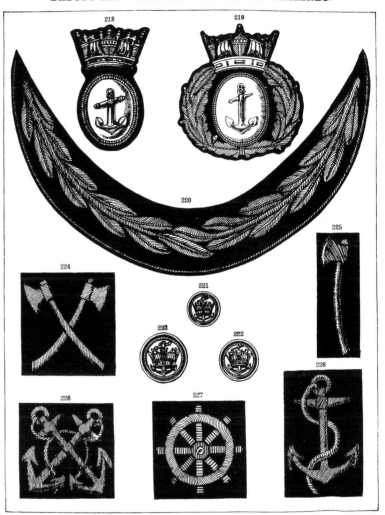

This illustration and the following one are pages from a catalogue produced by George Kenning & Son in the early 1930s. The key as to what was illustrated does not seem to have survived, but fortunately the principal badges can be identified as Canadian Pacific (132), Royal Mail (133), Lamport and Holt (137), and Nelson Line (139), with P&O still being available in 'sun' form (131) or 'sun and anchor' form (134), both with the sun having a face. Cunard is represented by (139).

This page from Kenning's catalogue gives some examples of Merchant Navy 'Standard' uniform elements that were available from this manufacturer. It shows in detail the small, medium and large button sizes as well as the laurel leaves on the peak of the master's cap and the oak leaves on the officer's cap badge.

Fifty-nine badges are family groups or revised or alternative badges. One is 'standard', that is, it is applicable to any shipping company, and eight are from training institutes (leaves, no. 230). Assuming that this is a representative collection, which seems plausible given that they have been collected and recorded in a haphazard way, then we can draw some interesting conclusions regarding the composition of these badges. In the main the central motif is surrounded by a wreath of plant material. In fact, 87 per cent of designs have laurel leaves, 7 per cent oak leaves, 1.3 per cent maple leaves, 0.8 per cent thistle and 0.8 per cent rice, although the rice is always shown in combination with laurel. Only 3.8 per cent of company cap badges have no wreath, such as the early P&O 'sun over anchor'.

Further examination reveals that 70 per cent of cap badges embody a flag, generally the company house flag, and 15 per cent include an anchor. This relative absence of anchors is interesting because not only does the 'standard' badge embody this motif, but an anchor was often used in some of the earliest examples of company badges including those used on sailing ships. Naval crowns surmount 21.5 per cent of cap badges. A further 10 per cent are surmounted by royal crowns, with an additional split of approximately one-third of the male form and two-thirds of the female although this probably only reflects the relative age of the specimens examined. The large majority, about 75 per cent of the cap badges examined, embody the flag of the company concerned. Flags made of cloisonné enamel account for 11.6 per cent of these. It is difficult to embroider an intricate flag with precision and using coloured enamel both improves the accuracy of the reproduction and improves the finished appearance of the badge. It must also impact on the cost of manufacture, but it is not known if this is a significant factor. What it does not do is improve the realism of the reproduction, as the cloisonné technique involves the use of bright metal partition lines to segregate the colours. Although this is very similar to the way that embroiderers use gold wire to form divisions and add brightness to the end product, the flags flown from the masthead of a ship don't really look the same.

More than half of the naval crowns employed on cap badges are made from pressed metal which is then gilded. This technique is also used for intricate emblems such as the Cunard lion, for example. Here the contours define the form of the object rather than there being any additional colour. Very occasionally the whole badge is made from pressed metal. In the sample examined in this study, 1.4 per cent fall into that category if one excludes the badge of the Manchester Ship Canal Company which is made from enamel.

By comparison, the Hawkins Collection of 564 cap badges held at Merseyside Maritime Museum includes 1.1 per cent of examples made from pressed metal if the badges of training institutions are excluded. It's therefore likely that this percentage of pressed metal badges is an accurate reflection of the numbers produced over time, although external factors could influence the use of the technique under certain circumstances. Pressed metal badges were, for example, used during the Second World War as an economy measure.

MAKING GOLD WIRE AND THREAD

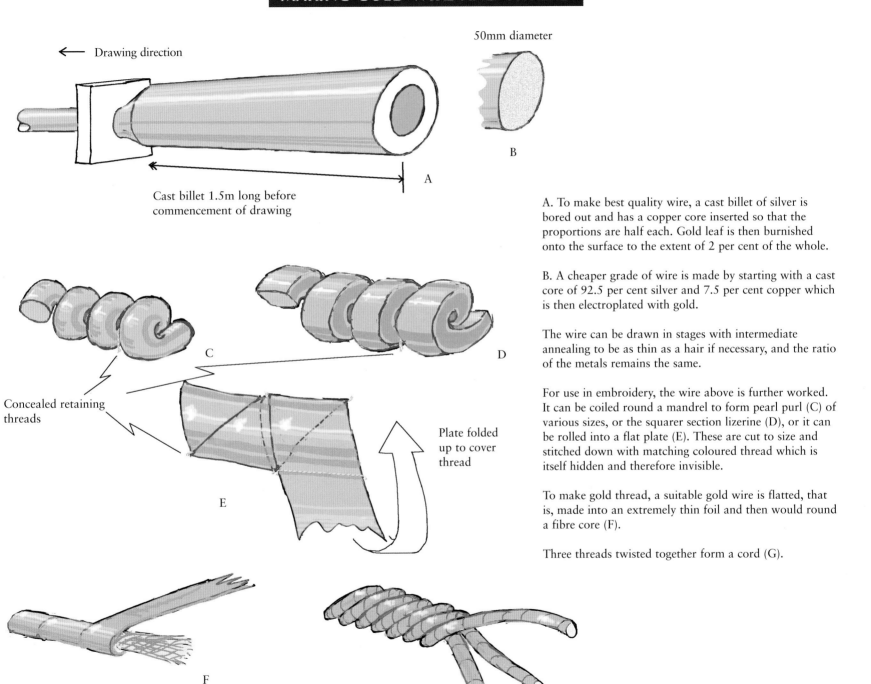

50mm diameter

← Drawing direction

Cast billet 1.5m long before commencement of drawing

A

B

Concealed retaining threads

C

D

Plate folded up to cover thread

E

F

G

A. To make best quality wire, a cast billet of silver is bored out and has a copper core inserted so that the proportions are half each. Gold leaf is then burnished onto the surface to the extent of 2 per cent of the whole.

B. A cheaper grade of wire is made by starting with a cast core of 92.5 per cent silver and 7.5 per cent copper which is then electroplated with gold.

The wire can be drawn in stages with intermediate annealing to be as thin as a hair if necessary, and the ratio of the metals remains the same.

For use in embroidery, the wire above is further worked. It can be coiled round a mandrel to form pearl purl (C) of various sizes, or the squarer section lizerine (D), or it can be rolled into a flat plate (E). These are cut to size and stitched down with matching coloured thread which is itself hidden and therefore invisible.

To make gold thread, a suitable gold wire is flatted, that is, made into an extremely thin foil and then would round a fibre core (F).

Three threads twisted together form a cord (G).

MANUFACTURE OF CAP BADGES

Illustrations 1 to 5 represent the types of production record of two badge manufacturers. The maker of the Cunard badge, illustrations 1 and 2, is unknown. Numbers 3, 4 and 5 illustrate the records kept by Stephen Simpson, although relating to two separate badges. In the latter case, there was a record card with instructions and sample threads which supplemented the primary working tool, a perforated brass sheet shown in picture 5. This stencil was placed over the fabric and a stencil brush used to apply French chalk in the form of a paste. This produced a pattern to guide the embroideress as shown in illustration 6. The type of card shown in illustrations 1 and 2 is a combination of record card and stencil.

1. Aberdeen Line

2. Aberdeen and Commonwealth

3. Albyn Line

4. Alcoa Shipping

5. Alexandra Towing Co.

6. Algoma Central Marine

7. Anchor Brocklebank

8. Anchor Line

9. Andrew Weir Shipping

10. Anglo-American Telegraph Co.

11. Anglo Saxon Petroleum

12. Anglo Saxon Petroleum

13. ARC Marine

14. Asiatic SN Co.

15. Associated British Ports

16. Associated Container Transportation

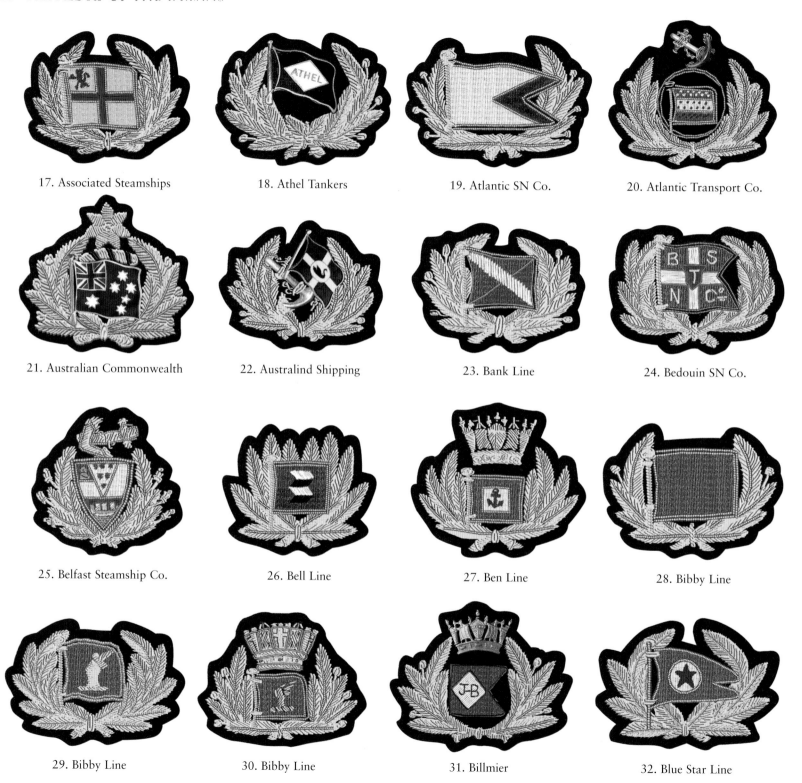

17. Associated Steamships

18. Athel Tankers

19. Atlantic SN Co.

20. Atlantic Transport Co.

21. Australian Commonwealth

22. Australind Shipping

23. Bank Line

24. Bedouin SN Co.

25. Belfast Steamship Co.

26. Bell Line

27. Ben Line

28. Bibby Line

29. Bibby Line

30. Bibby Line

31. Billmier

32. Blue Star Line

33. M.H. Bland & Co.

34. Blandford Shipping

35. Blandford Shipping

36. Booker Line

37. Booth Line

38. C.T. Bowring

39. British Africa SN Co.

40. British Antarctic Survey

41. British Channel Islands
Shipping Co.

42. British Channel
Island Ferries

43. Normandy Ferries

44. British & Commonwealth

45. British & Commonwealth
Petty Officer

46. British Columbia Ferries

47. British India

48. British & Irish SP Co.

49. B.P. Tanker Co.

50. Ministry of War Transport

51. British Phosphate
Commission

52. British Rail Seaspeed

53. British Tanker Co.

54. British Transport Docks Board

55. Bullard & King

56. Burmah Oil Co.

57. Burns & Laird

58. Burries Markes

59. Cairn Line

60. Caledonian MacBrayne

61. Caledonian Steam
Packet Company

62. Canadian Austrelasian Line

63. Canadian Coastguard

64. CN Marine

65. Canadian National Railways

66. Canadian National Steamships

67. CP Ships

68. Canadian Pacific Steamships

69. Canadian Pacific
Petty Officer

70. Canadian SS Lines

71. China Navigation

72. Clan Line

73. Clan Line

74. Coast Lines

75. Common Brothers

76. Commonwealth
Sugar Refiners

77. Wm Cory & Son

78. Crescent Shipping

79. Cunard

80. Cunard Petty Officer

81. Cunard

82. Cunard

83. Cunard

84. Cunard White Star
Petty Officer

85. J. & T. Brocklebank

86. Currie Line

87. Davies & Newman

88. J. & J. Denholm

89. Devitt & Moore

90. Dominion Line

91. Dundee, Perth & London
Shipping Co.

92. Eagle Oil & Shipping Co.

93. East African National
Shipping Line

94. East African Railways
& Harbours

95. Eastern Telegraph Co.

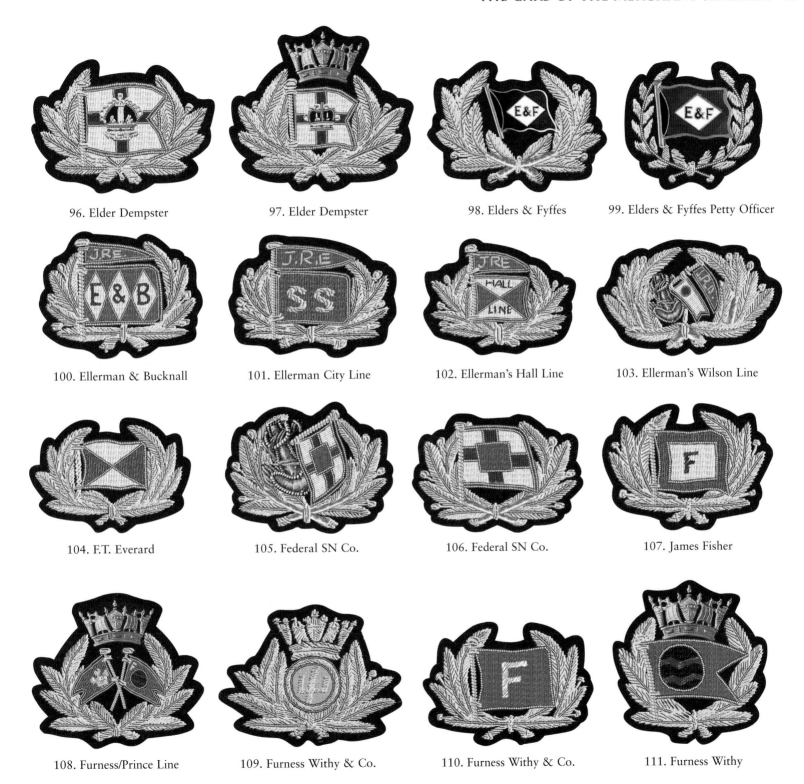

96. Elder Dempster

97. Elder Dempster

98. Elders & Fyffes

99. Elders & Fyffes Petty Officer

100. Ellerman & Bucknall

101. Ellerman City Line

102. Ellerman's Hall Line

103. Ellerman's Wilson Line

104. F.T. Everard

105. Federal SN Co.

106. Federal SN Co.

107. James Fisher

108. Furness/Prince Line

109. Furness Withy & Co.

110. Furness Withy & Co.

111. Furness Withy

112. Furness Withy Shipping

113. J. & G. Gardiner

114. GPO Cable Ships

115. GPO Cable Ships Petty Officer

116. General SN Co.

117. General SN Co.

118. Gilbert & Ellis Islands Marine

119. Great Eastern Railway

120. Glasgow Corporation

121. Glasgow & South Western Railway

122. Glen Line

123. Glen Line

124. Glen Line

125. Arthur Guinness

126. HM Coast Guard

127. HM Customs

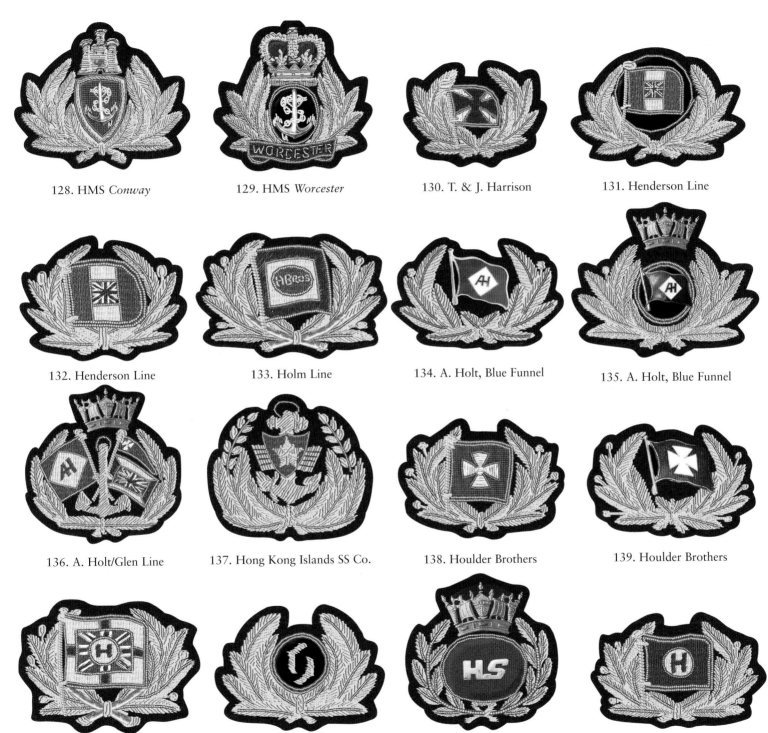

128. HMS *Conway*

129. HMS *Worcester*

130. T. & J. Harrison

131. Henderson Line

132. Henderson Line

133. Holm Line

134. A. Holt, Blue Funnel

135. A. Holt, Blue Funnel

136. A. Holt/Glen Line

137. Hong Kong Islands SS Co.

138. Houlder Brothers

139. Houlder Brothers

140. R.P. Houston

141. Hoverlloyd

142. Hoverspeed

143. Hudson SS Co.

144. Hudson's Bay Co.

145. Hull Gates Shipping

146. Hull Trinity House

147. Hunting & Son

148. Indo China SN Co.

149. International Maritime Carriers

150. Irish Shipping

151. Isle of Man SP Co.

152. Isle of Man SP Co.

153. Isle of Man SP Co.

154. Isle of Man SP
Co. Chief Steward

155. Jamaica Direct Fruit
Line Petty Officer

156. Kelly Shipping

157. Kiripati Marine

158. Lambert Brothers

159. Lambert Brothers

160. Lamport & Holt

161. Larinaga Steamship Co.

162. Lawther Lata

163. Leyland Line

164. Liverpool & North
Wales SS Co.

165. London Nautical College

166. Port of London Authority
Petty Officer

167. London & South Western Railway

168. Lobitos Oilfields

169. David MacBrayne

170. Manchester Liners

171. Manchester Ship Canal Co.

172. Manx Line

173. Manx Line

174. Marconi

175. McIlwraith & McEacharn

176. Merchant Navy
College Greenhythe

177. Merchant Navy Standard

178. MN Standard
Petty Officer

179. MN Standard (Bombay Style)

180. Mercury Shipping

181. Mersey Docks &
Harbour Board

182. R.W. Miller & Co.

183. Mobil Shipping

184. Mogul Line

185. M. Moss & Co.

186. Moss Hutchinson

187. Moss SS Co.

188. Nautilus SS Co.

189. Nelson Line

190. NZ Department of Railways

191. New Zealand Shipping Co.

192. New Zealand
Shipping Co./Federal

193. Nigerian Black Star

194. North of Scotland,
Orkney & Shetland

195. North Sea Ferries

196. Commissioners
of Northern Lights

197. Northern SS Co.

198. James Nourse

199. Ocean Cruise Line

200. Ocean Fleets

201. Orient Line

202. Orient Line

203. Orient Line Chief Steward

204. Overseas Containers Ltd

205. Pacific SN Co.

206. Palm Line

207. Palm Line Petty Officer

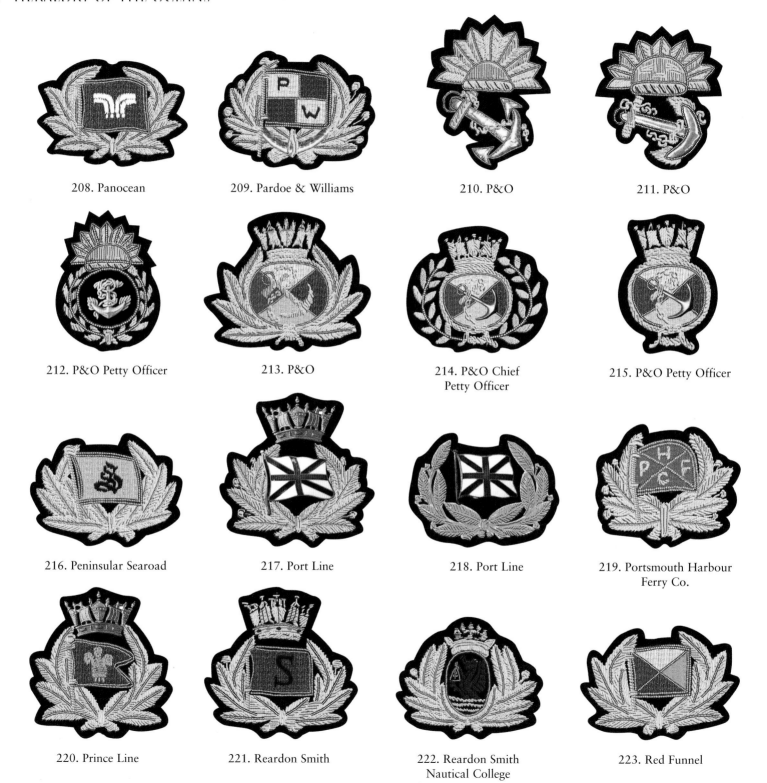

208. Panocean

209. Pardoe & Williams

210. P&O

211. P&O

212. P&O Petty Officer

213. P&O

214. P&O Chief Petty Officer

215. P&O Petty Officer

216. Peninsular Searoad

217. Port Line

218. Port Line

219. Portsmouth Harbour Ferry Co.

220. Prince Line

221. Reardon Smith

222. Reardon Smith Nautical College

223. Red Funnel

223. Red Funnel Petty Officer

225. Ropner Shipping

226. Royal Army Service Corps

227. Royal Fleet Auxiliary

228. Royal Fleet Auxiliary

229. Royal Maritime
Auxiliary Service

230. RMS *Wray Castle*

231. Royal National Lifeboat
Institution Coxwain

232. RNLI Crew

232. RNLI Mechanic

234. Royal Mail Line

235. Royal Mail Line

236. Royal Mail SP Co.

237. Royal Mail Line
Petty Officer

238. Royal Mail/PSN Co.

239. Royal Mail/PSN Co.
Petty Officer

240. Royal Naval Reserve

241. RN Transport

242. C. Rowbotham & Son

243. Walter Runciman

244. Sail Training Assoc.

245. Safmarine

246. Saguenay Shipping

247. Christian Salvesen

248. Scottish Ship Manager

249. Sealink Newhaven

250. Sealink British Ferries

251. Sealion

252. Seaspeed Purserette

253. Seaspeed Purserette

254. Sheaf S. Shipping Co.

255. Shaw Savill & Co.

256. Shaw, Savill & Albion

257. Shaw Savill/Aberdeen &
Commonwealth Petty Officer

258. Silver Line

259. Solent Aggregates

260. South African
Transport Service

261. South American
Saint Line

262. Southern Railway

263. Southampton Pilots

264. Stag Line

265. Strick Line

266. Sugar Line

267. Thompson S. Shipping

268. Thoresen Viking Ferries

269. Townsend Thoresen Ferries

270. TS *Mercury*

271. Trinder Anderson

272. Trident Tankers

273. Trinity House Cutter

274. Trinity House Elder Brother

275. Trinity House Elder Brother

276. Trinity House Officer

277. Trinity House Petty Officer

277. Trinity House

279. Turnbull Scott

280. Unicorn Line

281. Union Line

282. Union-Castle Line

283. Union-Castle Line
Petty Officer

284. Union SS Co. of
New Zealand

285. United Africa Co.

286. United Baltic Cpn

287. Upper Lakes Group

288. Warsash School of Navigation

289. Watts, Watts & Co.

290. West Hartlepool SN Co.

291. Westcott & Laurence

292. White Star Line

293. White Star Petty Officer

294. White Star Steward

295. White Star Porter

296. Wilson Line

297. Yeoward Brothers

Tinted daguerreotype *c.* 1850.
This depicts either Captain Philip Matthews Woolcott or his brother Commander John Henry Woolcott. The former worked for the Royal Mail Steam Packet Co. and the latter for the Pacific Steam Navigation Co. Unfortunately today the answer to this riddle is lost. (Reproduced by permission of the Dorset History Centre, reference D/MAR/F23)

298. Coast Guard by Gieves (reproduced courtesy of the Gieves & Hawkes Archives, 1 Saville Row, London, W1)

MEDALS WORN ON THE RIGHT BREAST

Royal National Lifeboat Institution
Lloyd's Medal for Saving Life at Sea
Shipwrecked Fishermen & Mariners Royal Benevolent Soc.
Liverpool Shipwreck and Humane Society
Royal Humane Society Silver Medal
Royal Humane Society Bronze Medal
Royal Humane Society Stanhope Medal
Lloyd's Medal for Meritorious Service
Lloyd's War Medal for Bravery at Sea
Merchant Navy Medal
Sea Gallantry Medal
Albert Medal (Gold)/George Cross
Albert Medal/George Medal
Transport Medal/Mercantile Marine Medal
Royal Naval Reserve Decoration
RNR Long Service & Good Conduct Medal
ME Order of the British Empire
Empire Gallantry Medal/George Cross
1914–1915 Star
British War Medal
Victory Medal
Victoria Cross
Distinguished Service Cross
Distinguished Service Medal
Conspicuous Gallantry Medal
Distinguished Service Order
1939–1945 War Medal
1939–1945 Star
Atlantic Star
Africa Star
Pacific Star
Burma Star
Italy Star
France and Germany Star
Naval General Service Medal Palestine/Cyprus/Suez
British Korea Medal
Naval General Service Medal Borneo
South Atlantic Medal
Gulf Medal
Arctic Star

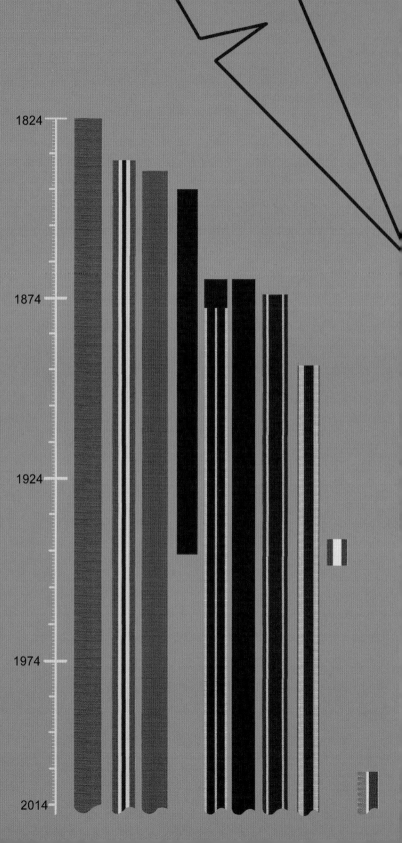

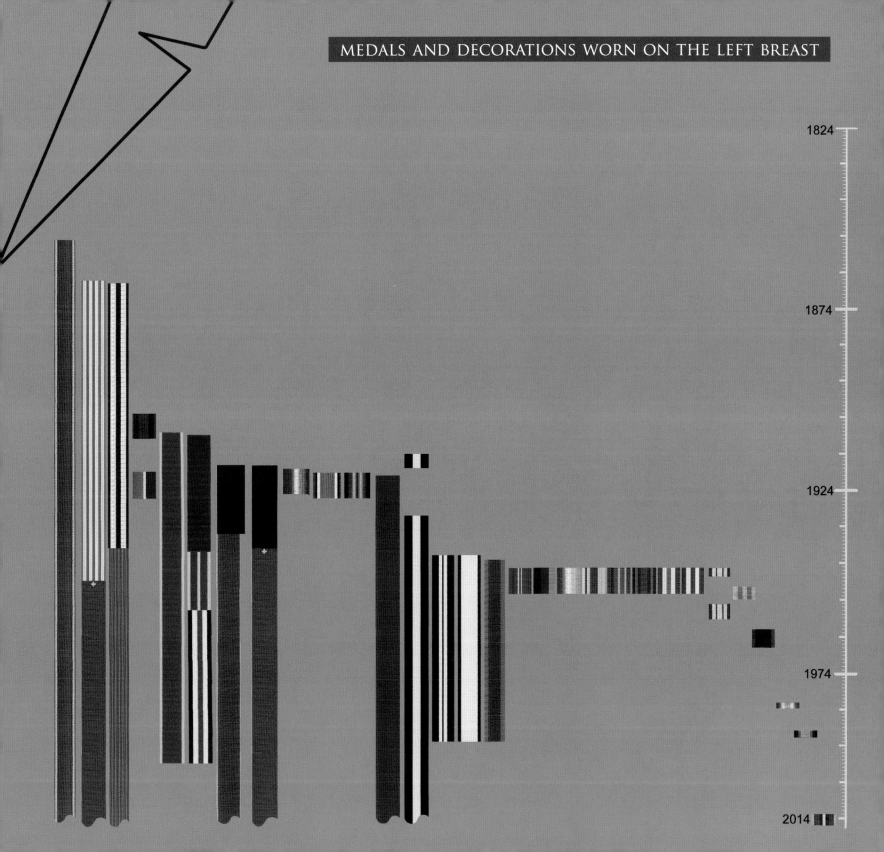

1824

1874

1924

1974

2014

ROYAL MAIL STEAM PACKET CO. UNIFORM REGULATIONS 1860

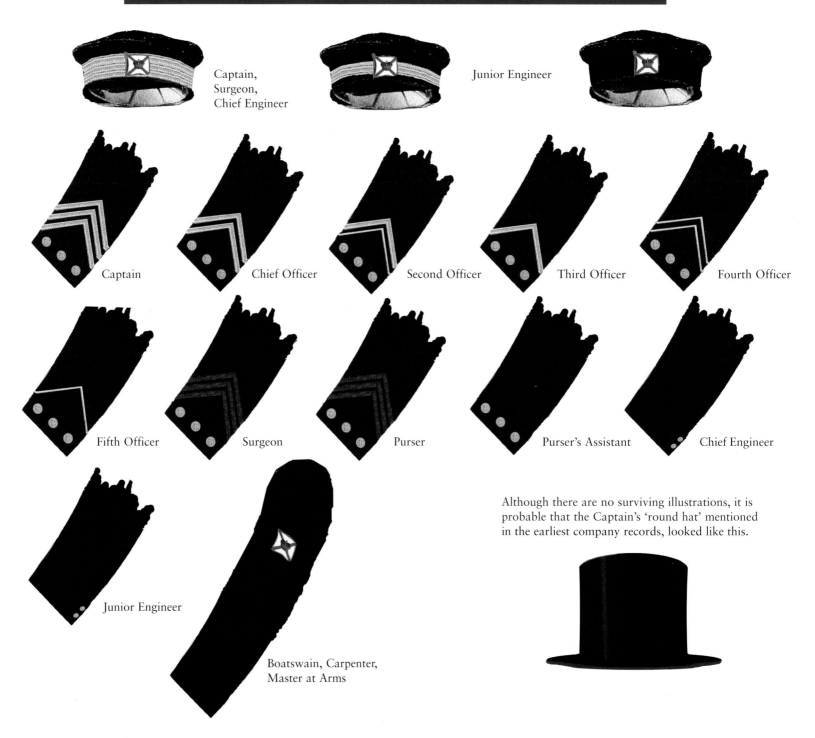

Captain,
Surgeon,
Chief Engineer

Junior Engineer

Captain

Chief Officer

Second Officer

Third Officer

Fourth Officer

Fifth Officer

Surgeon

Purser

Purser's Assistant

Chief Engineer

Junior Engineer

Boatswain, Carpenter,
Master at Arms

Although there are no surviving illustrations, it is probable that the Captain's 'round hat' mentioned in the earliest company records, looked like this.

P. & O. UNIFORM REGULATIONS 1869

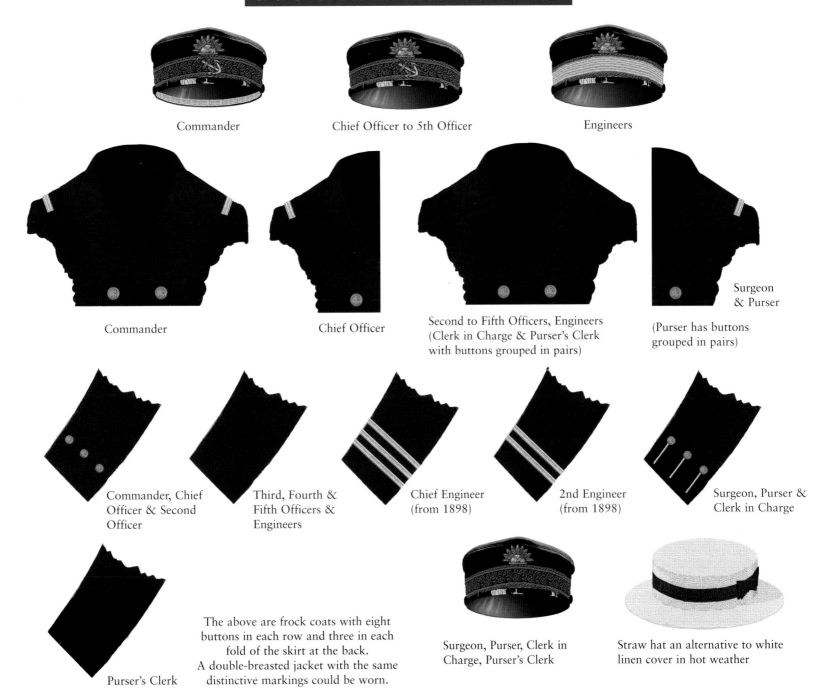

Commander

Chief Officer to 5th Officer

Engineers

Commander

Chief Officer

Second to Fifth Officers, Engineers
(Clerk in Charge & Purser's Clerk
with buttons grouped in pairs)

Surgeon
& Purser

(Purser has buttons
grouped in pairs)

Commander, Chief
Officer & Second
Officer

Third, Fourth &
Fifth Officers &
Engineers

Chief Engineer
(from 1898)

2nd Engineer
(from 1898)

Surgeon, Purser &
Clerk in Charge

Purser's Clerk

The above are frock coats with eight
buttons in each row and three in each
fold of the skirt at the back.
A double-breasted jacket with the same
distinctive markings could be worn.

Surgeon, Purser, Clerk in
Charge, Purser's Clerk

Straw hat an alternative to white
linen cover in hot weather

MERCHANT NAVY STANDARD UNIFORM 1919

The Union-Castle Regulations for 1950
adhere very closely to standard uniform.
The lace and titles used are identified in red.
Additional lace deviating from the standard
pattern is shown on p. 69. White covers
were worn.

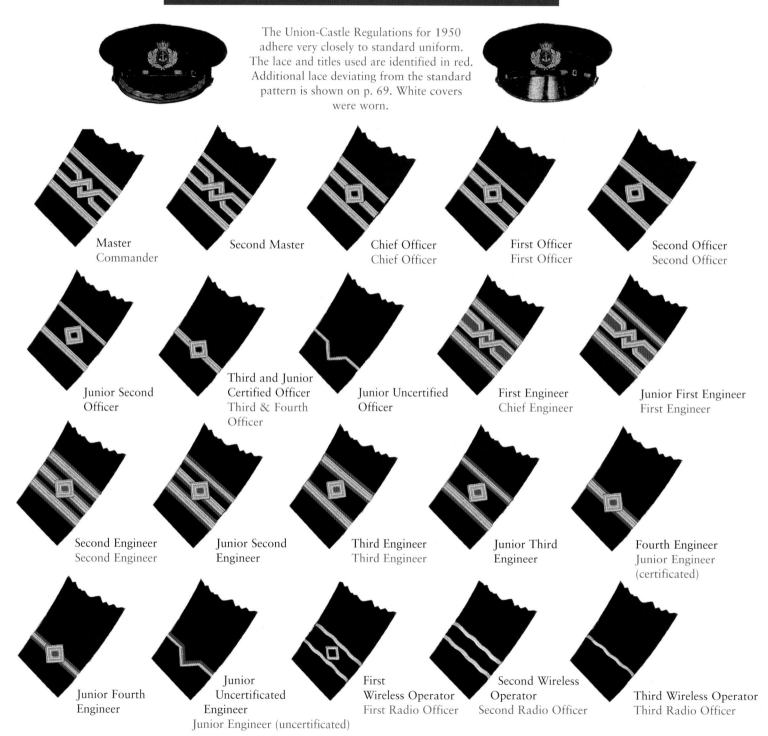

Master
Commander

Second Master

Chief Officer
Chief Officer

First Officer
First Officer

Second Officer
Second Officer

Junior Second
Officer

Third and Junior
Certified Officer
Third & Fourth
Officer

Junior Uncertified
Officer

First Engineer
Chief Engineer

Junior First Engineer
First Engineer

Second Engineer
Second Engineer

Junior Second
Engineer

Third Engineer
Third Engineer

Junior Third
Engineer

Fourth Engineer
Junior Engineer
(certificated)

Junior Fourth
Engineer

Junior
Uncertificated
Engineer
Junior Engineer (uncertificated)

First
Wireless Operator
First Radio Officer

Second Wireless
Operator
Second Radio Officer

Third Wireless Operator
Third Radio Officer

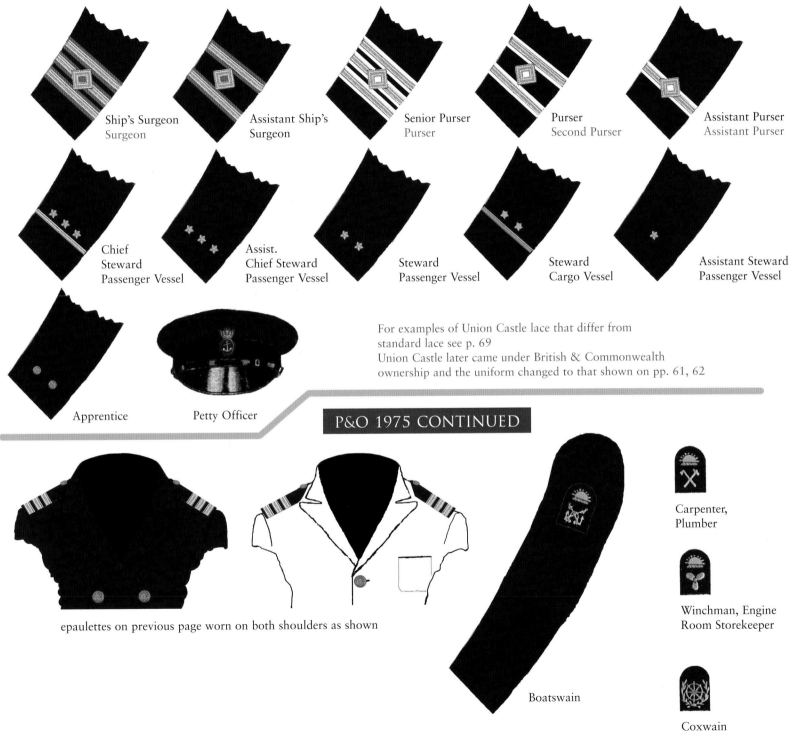

Ship's Surgeon
Surgeon

Assistant Ship's
Surgeon

Senior Purser
Purser

Purser
Second Purser

Assistant Purser
Assistant Purser

Chief
Steward
Passenger Vessel

Assist.
Chief Steward
Passenger Vessel

Steward
Passenger Vessel

Steward
Cargo Vessel

Assistant Steward
Passenger Vessel

Apprentice

Petty Officer

For examples of Union Castle lace that differ from
standard lace see p. 69
Union Castle later came under British & Commonwealth
ownership and the uniform changed to that shown on pp. 61, 62

P&O 1975 CONTINUED

epaulettes on previous page worn on both shoulders as shown

Carpenter,
Plumber

Winchman, Engine
Room Storekeeper

Boatswain

Coxwain

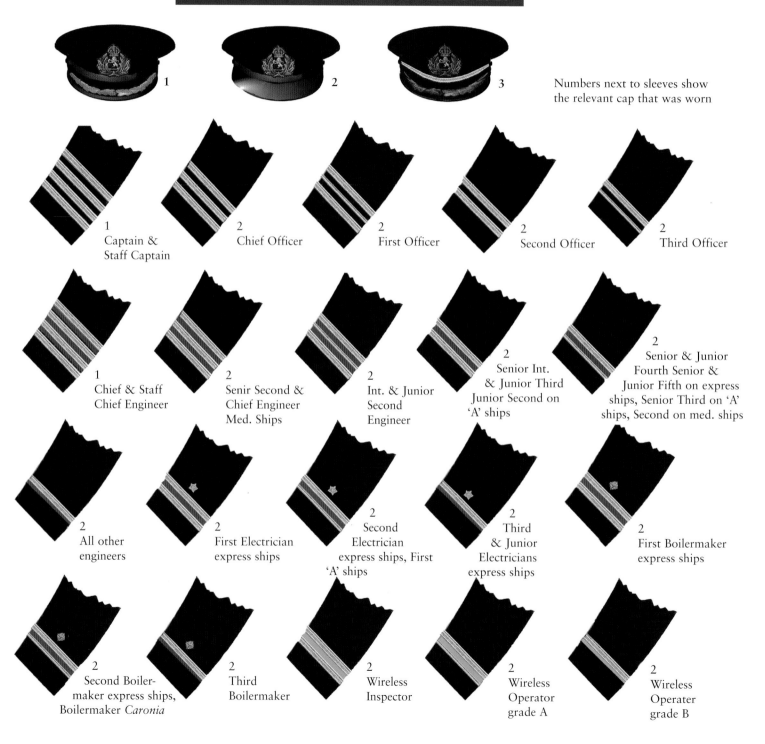

CUNARD UNIFORM REGULATIONS 1927

Numbers next to sleeves show
the relevant cap that was worn

1
Captain &
Staff Captain

2
Chief Officer

2
First Officer

2
Second Officer

2
Third Officer

1
Chief & Staff
Chief Engineer

2
Senir Second &
Chief Engineer
Med. Ships

2
Int. & Junior
Second
Engineer

2
Senior Int.
& Junior Third
Junior Second on
'A' ships

2
Senior & Junior
Fourth Senior &
Junior Fifth on express
ships, Senior Third on 'A'
ships, Second on med. ships

2
All other
engineers

2
First Electrician
express ships

2
Second
Electrician
express ships, First
'A' ships

2
Third
& Junior
Electricians
express ships

2
First Boilermaker
express ships

2
Second Boiler-
maker express ships,
Boilermaker *Caronia*

2
Third
Boilermaker

2
Wireless
Inspector

2
Wireless
Operator
grade A

2
Wireless
Operater
grade B

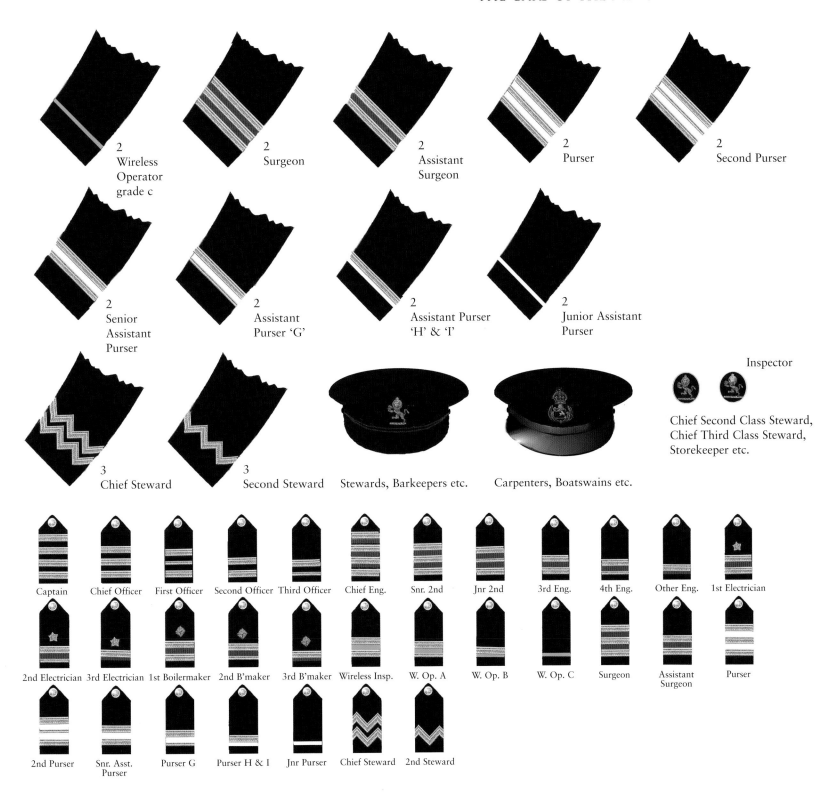

2 Wireless Operator grade c

2 Surgeon

2 Assistant Surgeon

2 Purser

2 Second Purser

2 Senior Assistant Purser

2 Assistant Purser 'G'

2 Assistant Purser 'H' & 'I'

2 Junior Assistant Purser

3 Chief Steward

3 Second Steward

Stewards, Barkeepers etc.

Carpenters, Boatswains etc.

Inspector

Chief Second Class Steward, Chief Third Class Steward, Storekeeper etc.

Captain

Chief Officer

First Officer

Second Officer

Third Officer

Chief Eng.

Snr. 2nd

Jnr 2nd

3rd Eng.

4th Eng.

Other Eng.

1st Electrician

2nd Electrician

3rd Electrician

1st Boilermaker

2nd B'maker

3rd B'maker

Wireless Insp.

W. Op. A

W. Op. B

W. Op. C

Surgeon

Assistant Surgeon

Purser

2nd Purser

Snr. Asst. Purser

Purser G

Purser H & I

Jnr Purser

Chief Steward

2nd Steward

CANADIAN PACIFIC UNIFORM REGULATIONS 1930

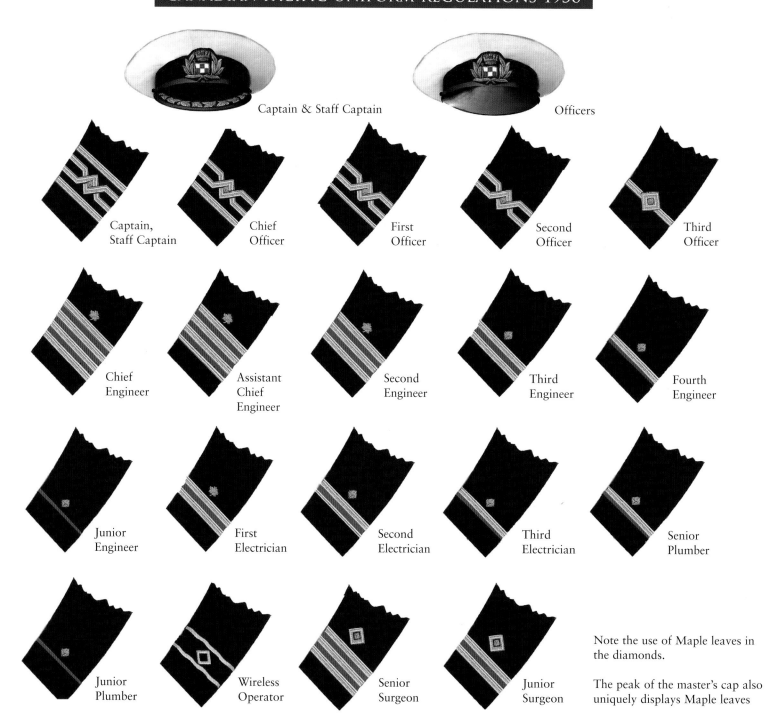

Captain & Staff Captain

Officers

Captain, Staff Captain

Chief Officer

First Officer

Second Officer

Third Officer

Chief Engineer

Assistant Chief Engineer

Second Engineer

Third Engineer

Fourth Engineer

Junior Engineer

First Electrician

Second Electrician

Third Electrician

Senior Plumber

Junior Plumber

Wireless Operator

Senior Surgeon

Junior Surgeon

Note the use of Maple leaves in the diamonds.

The peak of the master's cap also uniquely displays Maple leaves

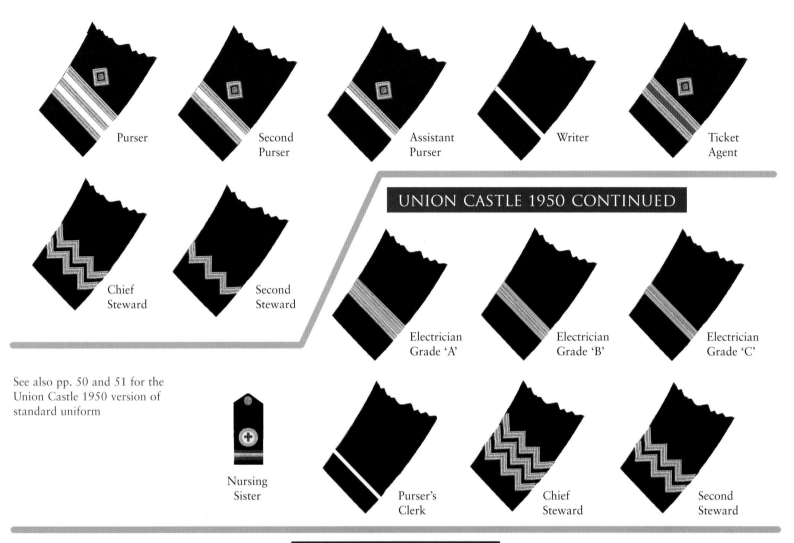

Purser

Second Purser

Assistant Purser

Writer

Ticket Agent

UNION CASTLE 1950 CONTINUED

Chief Steward

Second Steward

Electrician Grade 'A'

Electrician Grade 'B'

Electrician Grade 'C'

See also pp. 50 and 51 for the Union Castle 1950 version of standard uniform

Nursing Sister

Purser's Clerk

Chief Steward

Second Steward

P&O 1970 CONTINUED

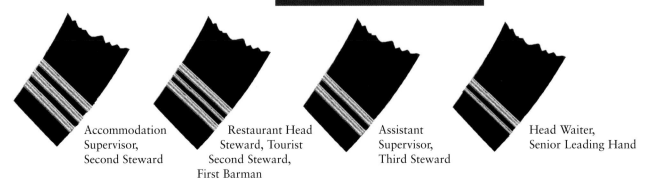

Accommodation Supervisor, Second Steward

Restaurant Head Steward, Tourist Second Steward, First Barman

Assistant Supervisor, Third Steward

Head Waiter, Senior Leading Hand

BRITISH INDIA SN CO. UNIFORM REGULATIONS 1949

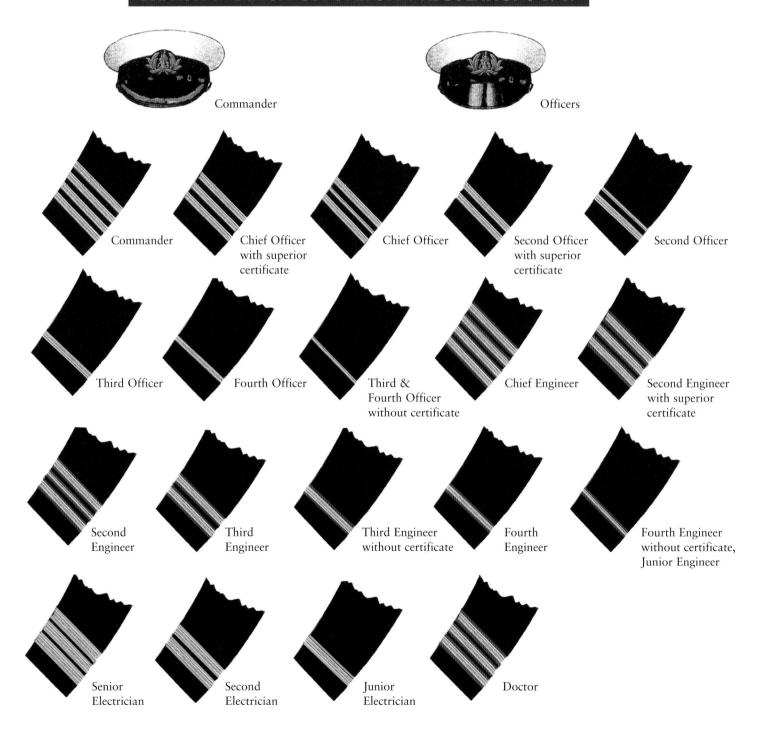

Commander

Officers

Commander

Chief Officer
with superior
certificate

Chief Officer

Second Officer
with superior
certificate

Second Officer

Third Officer

Fourth Officer

Third &
Fourth Officer
without certificate

Chief Engineer

Second Engineer
with superior
certificate

Second
Engineer

Third
Engineer

Third Engineer
without certificate

Fourth
Engineer

Fourth Engineer
without certificate,
Junior Engineer

Senior
Electrician

Second
Electrician

Junior
Electrician

Doctor

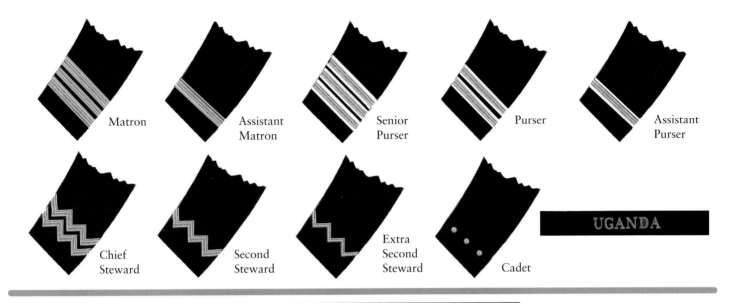

Matron

Assistant Matron

Senior Purser

Purser

Assistant Purser

Chief Steward

Second Steward

Extra Second Steward

Cadet

UGANDA

ROYAL MAIL LINE 1950 CONTINUED

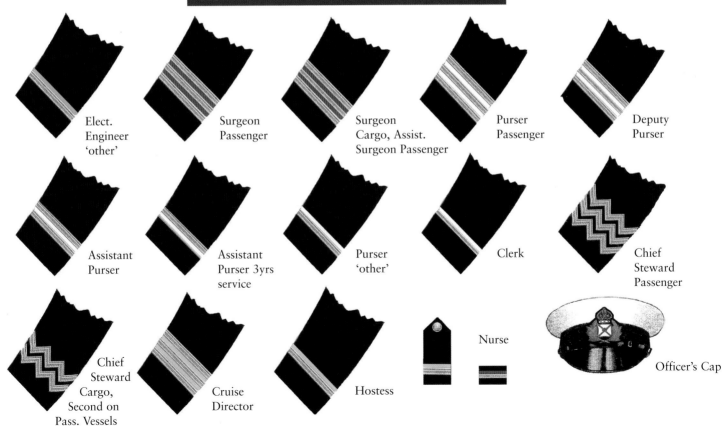

Elect. Engineer 'other'

Surgeon Passenger

Surgeon Cargo, Assist. Surgeon Passenger

Purser Passenger

Deputy Purser

Assistant Purser

Assistant Purser 3yrs service

Purser 'other'

Clerk

Chief Steward Passenger

Chief Steward Cargo, Second on Pass. Vessels

Cruise Director

Hostess

Nurse

Officer's Cap

ROYAL MAIL LINE UNIFORM REGULATIONS 1950

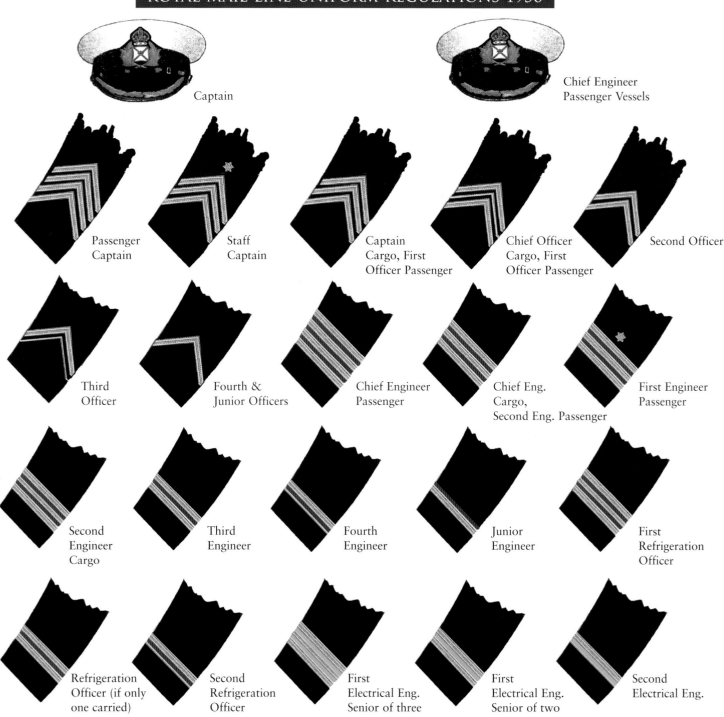

Captain

Chief Engineer
Passenger Vessels

Passenger
Captain

Staff
Captain

Captain
Cargo, First
Officer Passenger

Chief Officer
Cargo, First
Officer Passenger

Second Officer

Third
Officer

Fourth &
Junior Officers

Chief Engineer
Passenger

Chief Eng.
Cargo,
Second Eng. Passenger

First Engineer
Passenger

Second
Engineer
Cargo

Third
Engineer

Fourth
Engineer

Junior
Engineer

First
Refrigeration
Officer

Refrigeration
Officer (if only
one carried)

Second
Refrigeration
Officer

First
Electrical Eng.
Senior of three

First
Electrical Eng.
Senior of two

Second
Electrical Eng.

ORIENT LINE UNIFORM REGULATIONS 1960

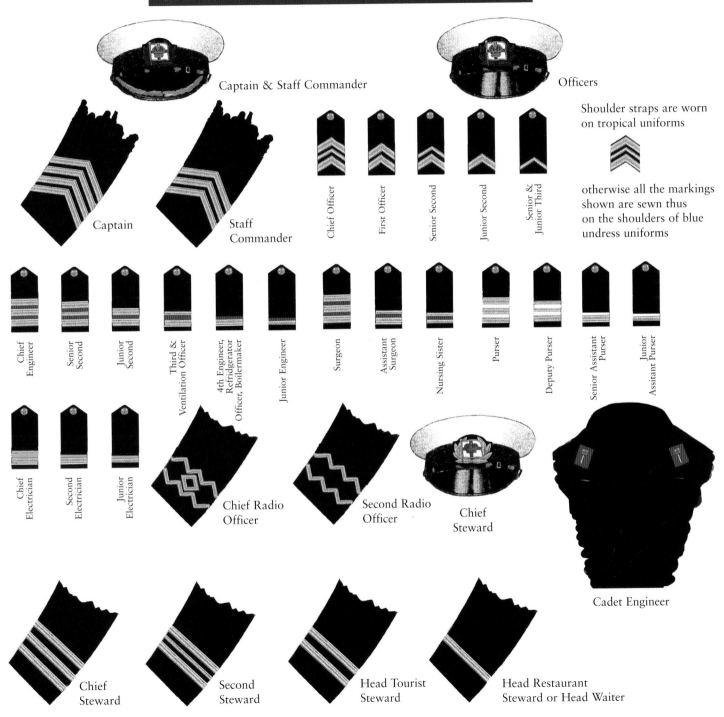

Captain & Staff Commander

Officers

Shoulder straps are worn on tropical uniforms

otherwise all the markings shown are sewn thus on the shoulders of blue undress uniforms

Captain

Staff Commander

Chief Officer

First Officer

Senior Second

Junior Second

Senior & Junior Third

Chief Engineer

Senior Second

Junior Second

Third & Ventilation Officer

4th Engineer, Refridgerator Officer, Boilermaker

Junior Engineer

Surgeon

Assistant Surgeon

Nursing Sister

Purser

Deputy Purser

Senior Assistant Purser

Junior Assitant Purser

Chief Electrician

Second Electrician

Junior Electrician

Chief Radio Officer

Second Radio Officer

Chief Steward

Cadet Engineer

Chief Steward

Second Steward

Head Tourist Steward

Head Restaurant Steward or Head Waiter

P&O UNIFORM REGULATIONS 1970

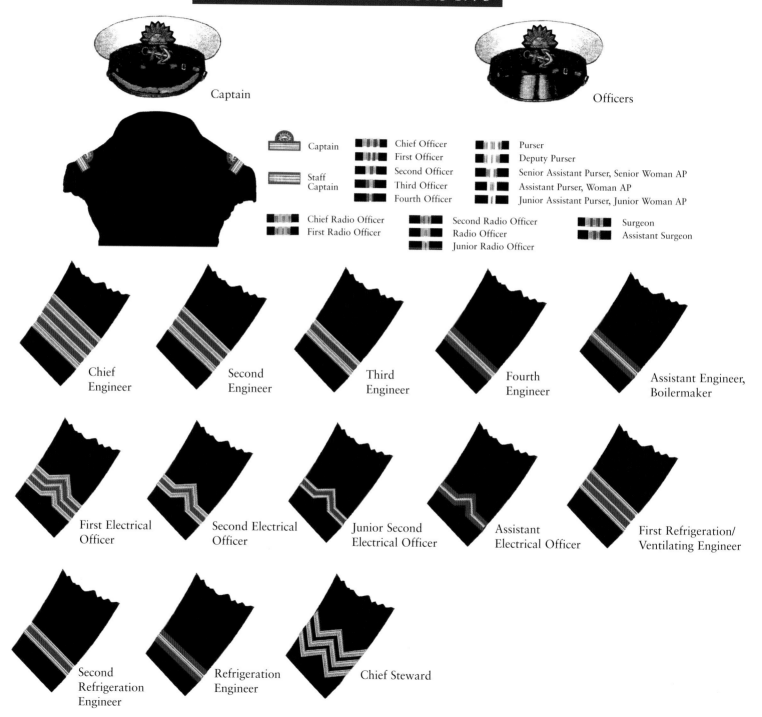

Captain

Officers

Captain

Staff Captain

Chief Officer
First Officer
Second Officer
Third Officer
Fourth Officer

Purser
Deputy Purser
Senior Assistant Purser, Senior Woman AP
Assistant Purser, Woman AP
Junior Assistant Purser, Junior Woman AP

Chief Radio Officer
First Radio Officer

Second Radio Officer
Radio Officer
Junior Radio Officer

Surgeon
Assistant Surgeon

Chief Engineer

Second Engineer

Third Engineer

Fourth Engineer

Assistant Engineer, Boilermaker

First Electrical Officer

Second Electrical Officer

Junior Second Electrical Officer

Assistant Electrical Officer

First Refrigeration/ Ventilating Engineer

Second Refrigeration Engineer

Refrigeration Engineer

Chief Steward

BRITISH & COMMONWEALTH UNIFORM REGULATIONS 1970

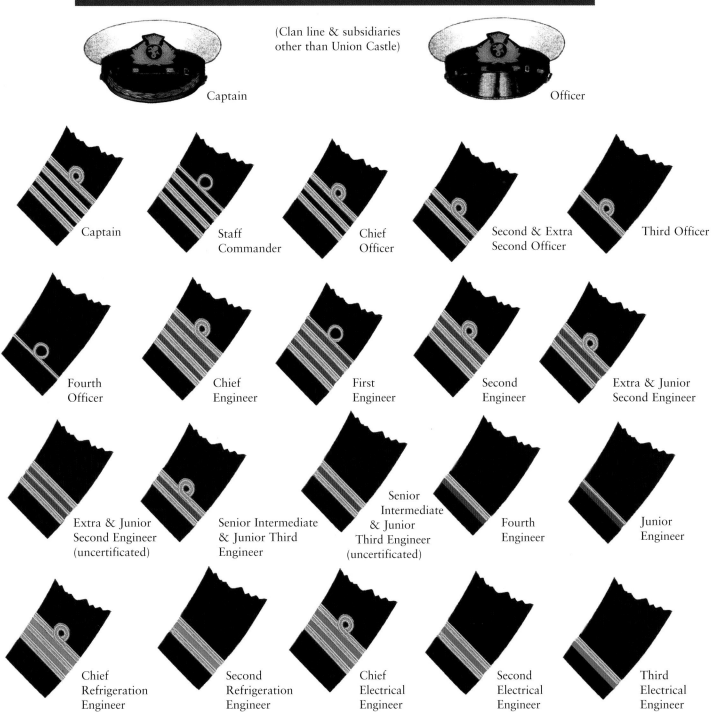

(Clan line & subsidiaries other than Union Castle)

Captain

Officer

Captain

Staff Commander

Chief Officer

Second & Extra Second Officer

Third Officer

Fourth Officer

Chief Engineer

First Engineer

Second Engineer

Extra & Junior Second Engineer

Extra & Junior Second Engineer (uncertificated)

Senior Intermediate & Junior Third Engineer

Senior Intermediate & Junior Third Engineer (uncertificated)

Fourth Engineer

Junior Engineer

Chief Refrigeration Engineer

Second Refrigeration Engineer

Chief Electrical Engineer

Second Electrical Engineer

Third Electrical Engineer

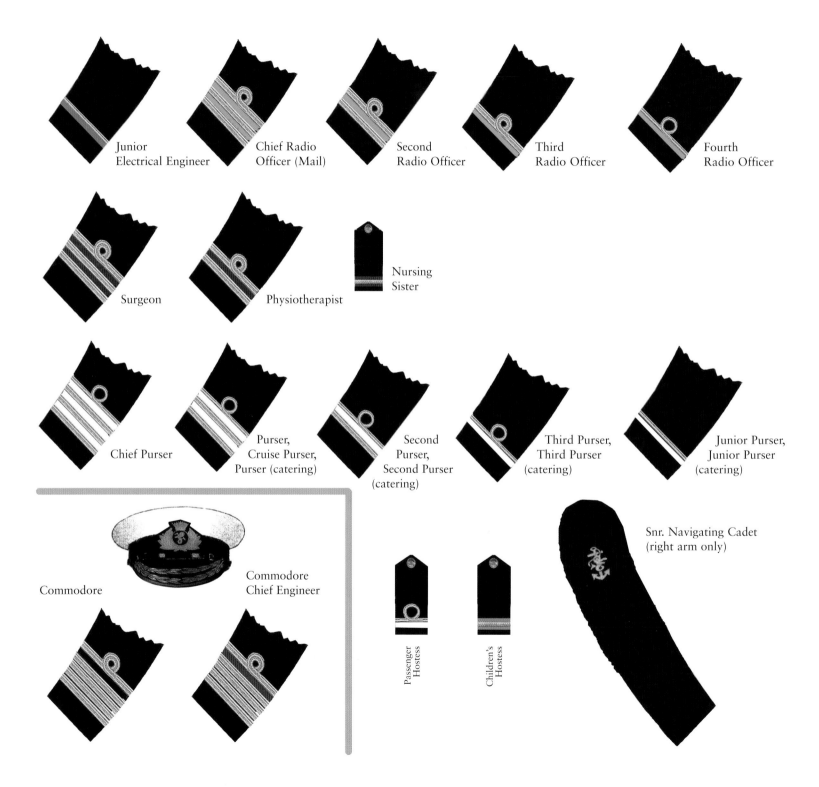

Junior
Electrical Engineer

Chief Radio
Officer (Mail)

Second
Radio Officer

Third
Radio Officer

Fourth
Radio Officer

Surgeon

Physiotherapist

Nursing
Sister

Chief Purser

Purser,
Cruise Purser,
Purser (catering)

Second
Purser,
Second Purser
(catering)

Third Purser,
Third Purser
(catering)

Junior Purser,
Junior Purser
(catering)

Commodore

Commodore
Chief Engineer

Passenger
Hostess

Children's
Hostess

Snr. Navigating Cadet
(right arm only)

P&O UNIFORM REGULATIONS

WITH BADGE DESIGN BY H. SPANTON AFTER AMALGAMATION WITH ORIENT LINE IN 1972

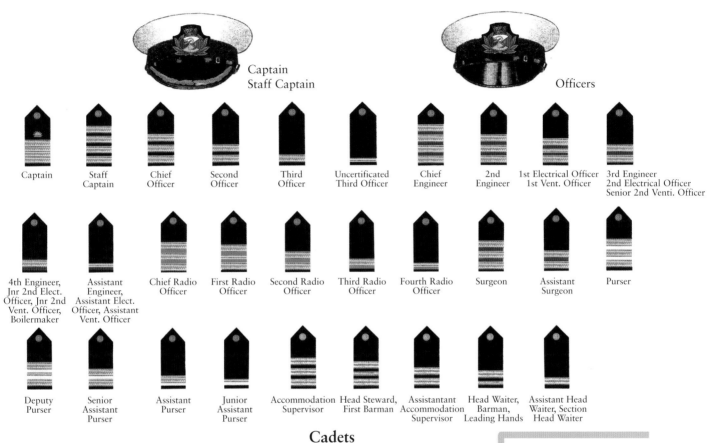

Captain
Staff Captain

Officers

Captain

Staff
Captain

Chief
Officer

Second
Officer

Third
Officer

Uncertificated
Third Officer

Chief
Engineer

2nd
Engineer

1st Electrical Officer
1st Vent. Officer

3rd Engineer
2nd Electrical Officer
Senior 2nd Venti. Officer

4th Engineer,
Jnr 2nd Elect.
Officer, Jnr 2nd
Vent. Officer,
Boilermaker

Assistant
Engineer,
Assistant Elect.
Officer, Assistant
Vent. Officer

Chief Radio
Officer

First Radio
Officer

Second Radio
Officer

Third Radio
Officer

Fourth Radio
Officer

Surgeon

Assistant
Surgeon

Purser

Deputy
Purser

Senior
Assistant
Purser

Assistant
Purser

Junior
Assistant
Purser

Accommodation
Supervisor

Head Steward,
First Barman

Assistantant
Accommodation
Supervisor

Head Waiter,
Barman,
Leading Hands

Assistant Head
Waiter, Section
Head Waiter

Cadets

Chief Petty Officer

Petty Officer

Purser

Navigation   Engineering

Commodore

CUNARD UNIFORM REGULATIONS 1980

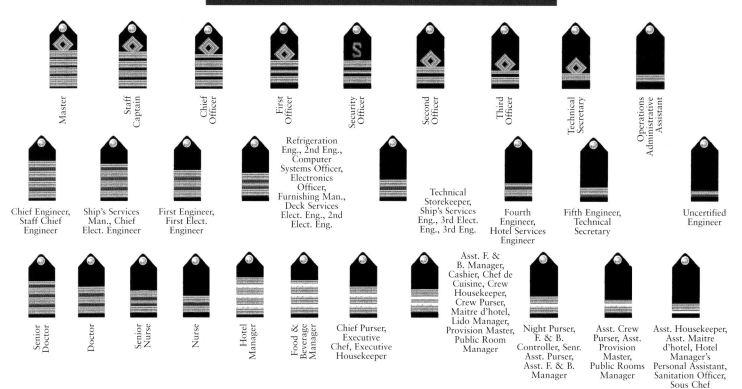

Master | Staff Captain | Chief Officer | First Officer | Security Officer | Second Officer | Third Officer | Technical Secretary | Operations Administrative Assistant

Chief Engineer, Staff Chief Engineer | Ship's Services Man., Chief Elect. Engineer | First Engineer, First Elect. Engineer | Refrigeration Eng., 2nd Eng., Computer Systems Officer, Electronics Officer, Furnishing Man., Deck Services Elect. Eng., 2nd Elect. Eng. | Technical Storekeeper, Ship's Services Eng., 3rd Elect. Eng., 3rd Eng. | Fourth Engineer, Hotel Services Engineer | Fifth Engineer, Technical Secretary | Uncertified Engineer

Senior Doctor | Doctor | Senior Nurse | Nurse | Hotel Manager | Food & Beverage Manager | Chief Purser, Executive Chef, Executive Housekeeper | Asst. F. & B. Manager, Cashier, Chef de Cuisine, Crew Housekeeper, Crew Purser, Maitre d'hotel, Lido Manager, Provision Master, Public Room Manager | Night Purser, F. & B. Controller, Senr. Asst. Purser, Asst. F. & B. Manager | Asst. Crew Purser, Asst. Provision Master, Public Rooms Manager | Asst. Housekeeper, Asst. Maitre d'hotel, Hotel Manager's Personal Assistant, Sanitation Officer, Sous Chef

London & South Western Railway *c.* 1890

Master | Mate | 2nd Mate

Federal SN Co. 1900

Master

Glasgow & South Western Railway Steamers

Master
(note direction of curl)

Caledonian Steam Packet Co.

Master

In this transitional period, some masters still wore rank distinction lace on the cap. Both these federal examples carry the new cap badge. See p. 33 for the old badge also still worn at this time.

WHITE STAR LINE

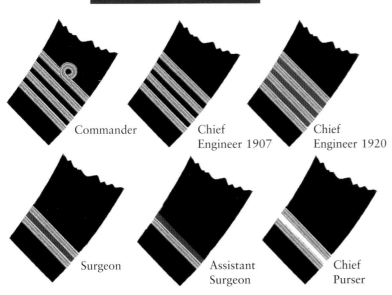

Commander

Chief Engineer 1907

Chief Engineer 1920

Surgeon

Assistant Surgeon

Chief Purser

White Star Regulations of 1907 required deck officers to have a curl and engineering officers to have straight lace. In both cases, ordinary reefer jackets had black mohair distinction lace. These examples would suit mess dress or great coats. Colours were only introduced after the First World War when straight lace was used throughout.

MARCONI

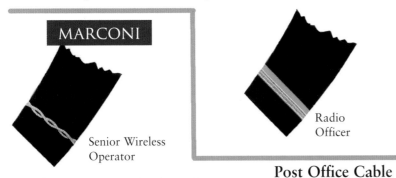

Senior Wireless Operator

Radio Officer

Amendment to Standard Uniform 1967

Post Office Cable Ships 1890

Chief Radio Officer

First Radio Officer

Chief Officer

WORLD WAR II

Battle Dress

Caps were of soft construction with a badge typically MN Standard, RNR or RNVR; otherwise a steel helmet was available.

The use of battledress persisted 'at wearer's option' until at least 1954 with Clan Line Steamers, Scottish Shire Line, British and South American SN Co. and associated companies.

Whatever the rank or form of lace, only half the sleeve was covered as an economy measure, rather than forming a complete circle.

An early Ordinary or Able-Bodied Seaman's leather belt with company insignia.

The female equivalent petersham ribbon belt of a nurse. In the twentieth century, many did not have company emblems.

Unusually, this sleeve marking of a police officer who is also a seaman, carries his number, so it is specific to an individual.

Examples of the development of tallies from the elaborate ship-centred woven silk of the 1890s to the printed synthetic material of the 1960s.

Badge awarded to merchant seamen and members of the fishing fleet who had been torpedoed or mined during the First World War.

RATINGS

Caledonian Steam Packet Co.
Ordinary Seaman *c.* 1890

U-C.M.S.Cº   16

I.W.S.P.Cº   17

WHITE STAR LINE   18

CUNARD   19

HOULDER LINE   20

L & N W S S Cº   21

THE NEW ZEALAND SHIPPING Cº   22

S.R.   23

Later use of guernseys by officers

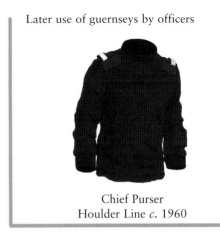

Chief Purser
Houlder Line *c.* 1960

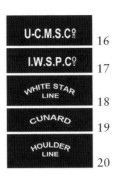

Badges for various grades of Rating in the Royal Navy were introduced in 1827, but varied widely. They only became standardised in 1879 when woven designs appeared.

DEMS   14

FBI   15

The Mercantile Marine Standard Uniform Committee stipulated the following distinguishing badges for Ratings or Petty Officers embroidered in either red or gilt when on a serge blue uniform, or in blue when on a cotton duck uniform:

1 Donkeyman or Chief Stoker, 2 Greaser or Leading Stoker, 3 Boatswain, 4 Boatswain's Mate, 5 Carpenter, 6 Carpenter's Mate, 7 Quartermaster and (not shown) a half wheel for an Assistant Quartermaster. Crossed hammers were also specified for a blacksmith or plumber and a single hammer for his assistant.

These were all worn on the left sleeve, half way between the elbow and the shoulder. Cunard used a crossed axe and a hammer for both the Carpenter and the Carpenter's Mate (12) as did the Anglo-American Telegraph Company.

FEMALE DRESS

Nurses would wear the badge of the institution where they trained and a linen square on the head (pinned on).

Occasionally Cunard lions are found on pinafores at this time.

White Star
Stewardess
1928

Cunard
Stewardess
1951

Orient Line
Sister
1952

P&O Purser
1967
(Hardy Amies)

Undress Coat or Reefer Jacket
with different styles of lace

Pattern of lace used by
Union Line in 1890s

Swimming
Instructress White
Star Line 1920s

Purserette North
Sea Ferries 1978
(International
Uniforms Ltd,
London)

Houlder Brothers 1900

White Star 1930

Here the wearer displays
medals of the First World
War including DSO

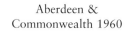

Aberdeen &
Commonwealth 1960

Here the wearer displays
medals of the Second
World War

Federal 1900

See also picture of Captain Woolcott on p. 45 for earlier style

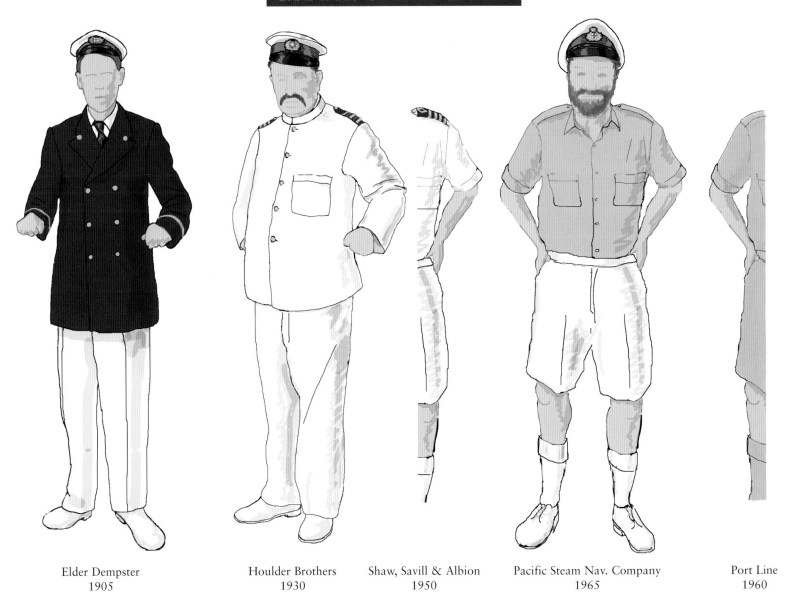

EXAMPLES OF TROPICAL KIT

Elder Dempster
1905

Houlder Brothers
1930

Shaw, Savill & Albion
1950

Pacific Steam Nav. Company
1965

Port Line
1960

See also the straw hat on p. 49, the singe-breasted jacket of 1975 on p. 51 and the seaman's blouse on p. 67 (this last-mentioned example is unusually worn over a guernsey).

The Cunard epaulettes shown on p. 53 were worn with the more formal type of tunic with an upstanding collar as illustrated for Houlder Brothers above. White trousers for home service had been discontinued by the Royal Navy in 1856. The Elder Dempster rig above illustrates tropical gear.

DRESS OF LASCARS AND SEEDIES

topi

Note the actual design of the embroidery would be arbitrary and variable. The particular pattern here is based on one used by P&O as a ceremonial uniform for Pakistani crew in 1992.

lalchi

rhumal

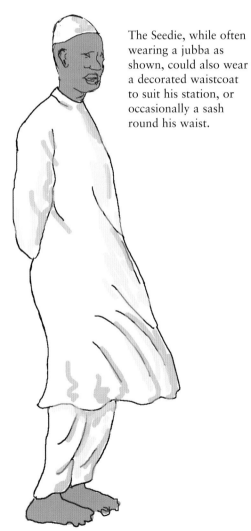

The Seedie, while often wearing a jubba as shown, could also wear a decorated waistcoat to suit his station, or occasionally a sash round his waist.

Among Lascars, particularly in P&O, the Khalassii has a plain red hat band and the Cassib, Paniwallah and Bhandary have none.

Serang and Tindal wear an embroidered lalchi, Bengal tartan rhumal and hat band, and have a boatswain's whistle on a silver chain about the neck as a badge of office.

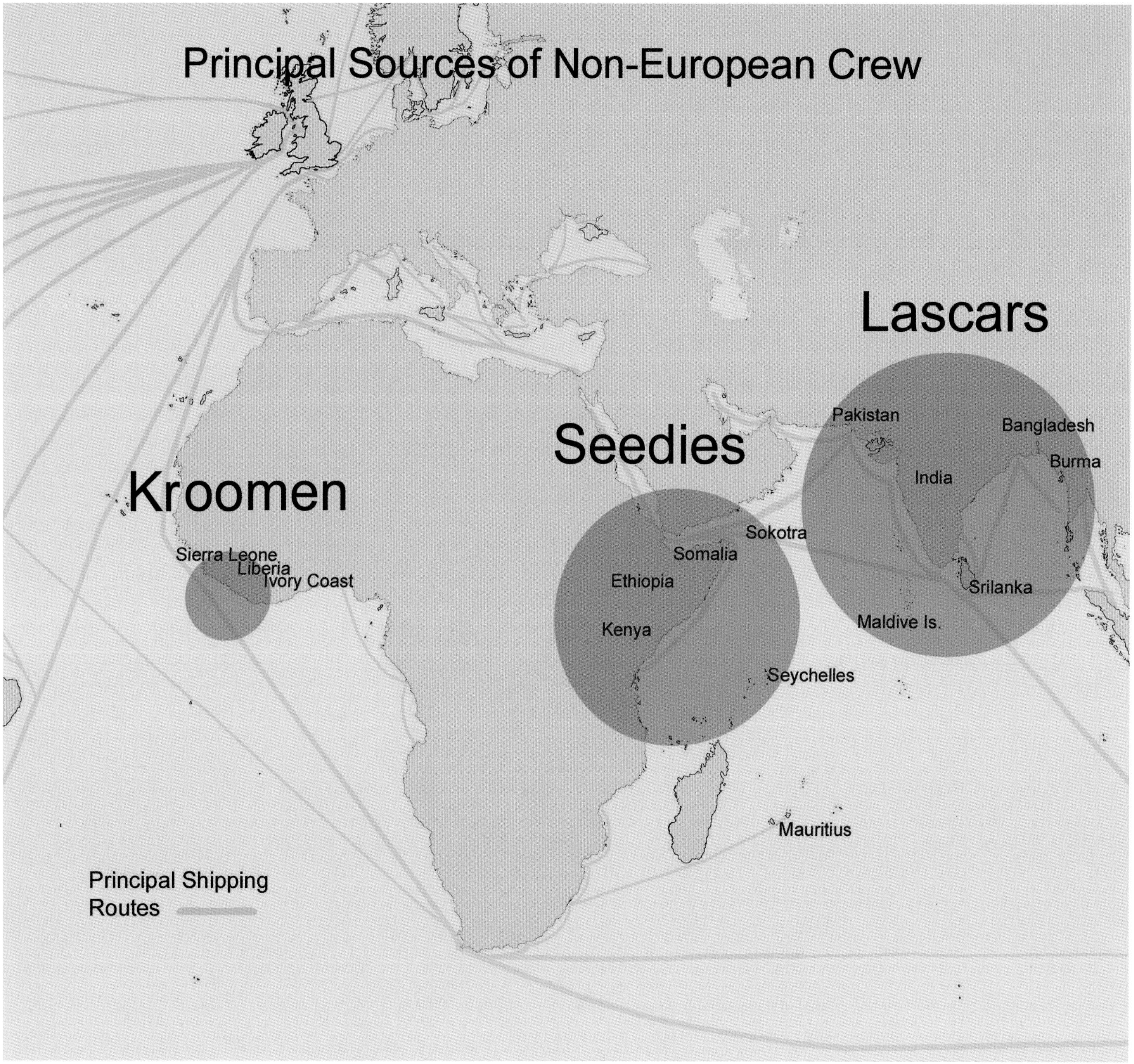

Principal Sources of Non-European Crew

Lascars

Seedies

Kroomen

Pakistan

Bangladesh

Burma

India

Sokotra

Somalia

Sierra Leone
Liberia
Ivory Coast

Ethiopia

Srilanka

Kenya

Maldive Is.

Seychelles

Mauritius

Principal Shipping
Routes

Motifs Drawn from the Vegetable Kingdom

Five types of leaf have been used to form the wreaths that surround the central motif on cap badges. By far the majority use the leaves of *Laurus nobilis*, the laurel or bay tree, an evergreen Mediterranean shrub that today is used in cooking but which in the ancient world was used for the circlets that crowned the victor in competition. Some badges, usually the smaller ones such as the standard Merchant Navy cap badge, use stylised oak leaves, which might represent strength or courage. A proportion of those badges representing Canadian companies include the native maple leaf.

The fourth plant, which because of its open structure is represented along with laurel leaves, is the rice plant (*Oryza sativa*) which has been used in a large percentage of cap badges from shipping companies based in Hong Kong. Use of the rice plant motif gives a characteristic height to such badges, as can be seen from the examples illustrated here as nos 137 and 149.

A few Scottish companies use thistle leaves as part of their badge, though this is hardly surprising as the thistle has been the national plant badge since at least the thirteenth century. An example of the use of thistle leaves is the badge of David MacBrayne, no. 169, which also embodies symbolic thistle flowers.

The first two plant motifs, laurel and oak, have been used as badges of distinction since ancient times. Laurel or bay featured prominently in Greek, Roman and Biblical culture and represents fame and triumph, while oak is emblematic of faith and endurance. The other plants used in this context are native flora in the countries where the companies who included them on their badges are, or were, based. Sometimes varying numbers of the fruiting bodies of the plants used as motifs, such as acorns or berries, are represented round the periphery of the design. Over the years two stylised forms of laurel berries have evolved, although nobody seems to know whether this represents the practice of different manufacturers or simply a change in the fashion of artistic representation.

Some Scottish companies follow Scottish heraldic practice by incorporating a 'motto scroll', a belt encircling a 'badge'. This style is considered to be appropriate both for corporate bodies as well as for individuals. Some companies surmount their cap badges with a royal or imperial crown. This changes in shape depending on whether the monarch of the day is a king or a queen. Some examples of both types are illustrated here, the companies concerned having been those involved in early mail contracts. Not all shipping lines were awarded this symbol. The badges of P&O and Union Line never carried a crown and the earliest Royal Mail Steam Packet Company cap badge was simply a representation of the house flag, which itself has a crown in the centre. Later badges were encircled by a laurel wreath and surmounted by a crown.

Telephone:
Avenue 6296.
Cables:
"Haysomite, London."

GEORGE SAMUEL HAYSOM, LTD.

MANUFACTURERS, GOVERNMENT AND SHIPPING CONTRACTORS.

Naval Outfitters.
Merchant Shippers.

Contractors to Principal Steam Ship Lines.

1-3, CREECHURCH LANE
Leadenhall St., LONDON,
And at Rotterdam. E.C. 3.

Haysom advertisement of 1924.

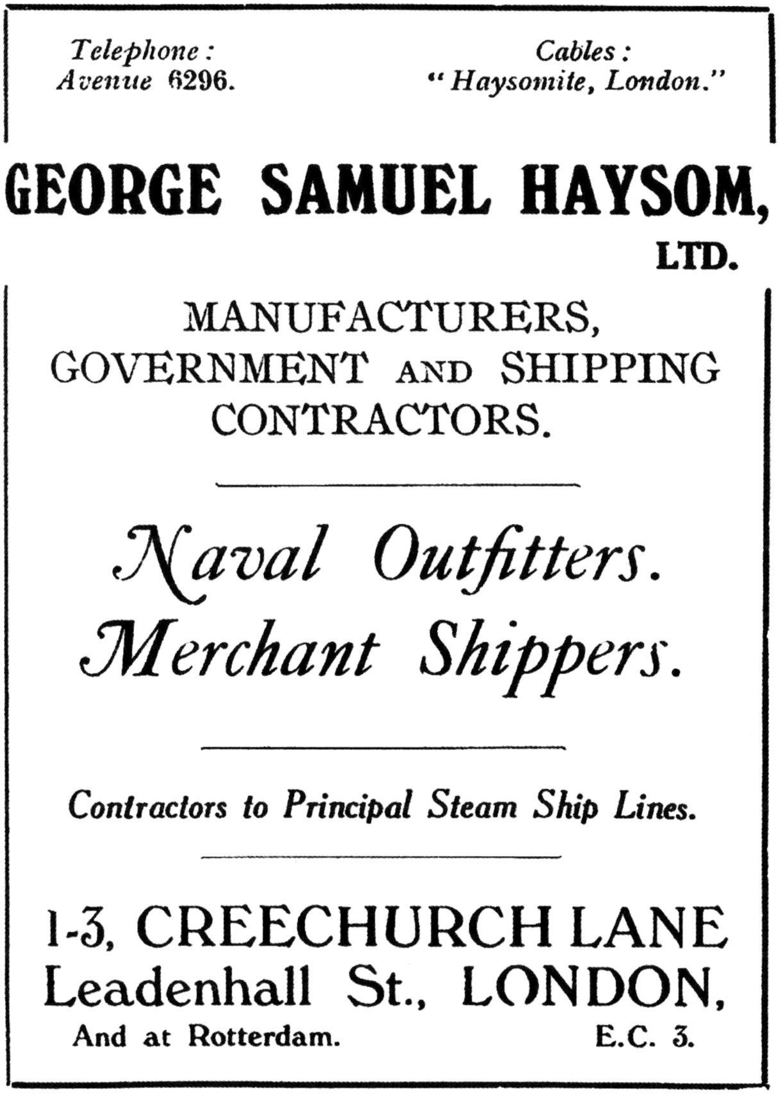

The Merchant Navy standard officers' cap badge has an oak leaf surround and is surmounted by a naval or Tudor crown. A different version, comprising the standard elements with a laurel wreath, is known as 'Bombay style' because tailors and merchant outfitters in that city, now Mumbai, offered it as a variation. Some seafarers may have had no choice in the matter of badge supplied if they were away from their home port for extended periods, while others may have appreciated the grander appearance of the 'Bombay' variant. In fact, manufacture was never restricted to the Indian subcontinent for this version was also listed on the online catalogue of the Canadian manufacturer, William Scully Lteé, in 2012 and as this style of badge was relatively common, most serious collectors of cap badges will probably have one.

There are examples of company cap badges illustrated here where there is a version with a naval crown and another otherwise identical badge without the crown. There appears to be no company-inspired reason for this. It does not differentiate officers from petty officers for example, rather it is a fashion item added on behalf of the wearer, perhaps to bestow gravitas. Use of these 'Bombay roses' would confer on the wearer the same apparent status as members of those fleets where the crown was part of the standard rig. Therefore we can see that, for officers at least, the merchant company cap badge has tended to grow in size over the years, starting simply with the company house flag or symbol and then surrounding it with a wreath and surmounting it with a crown. This increase in the sophistication of cap badges over time has also allowed the development of 'families' of cap badges in the larger fleets, where crews have tended to be large and with many separate and distinct roles among them. Variations of the company cap badge can be exemplified by the Cunard 'family' which in the 1920s comprised a set of badges for, in descending order of ornament, Officers, Carpenters and Boatswains, First Class Stewards and Bookkeepers, Second and Third Class Stewards and Storekeepers, and Inspectors. Another 'family' was that of the post-1972 P&O series of badges comprising Officer, Chief Petty Officer and Petty Officer.

Other companies have differentiated roles by changing the colour of the surrounding wreath, for example on the badges used by Orient Line, where the normally black Officer's wreath became silver for the Chief Steward. The Petty Officers and Ratings badge was surrounded by a light blue laurel wreath. The 1947 Orient Line Regulations stipulate that the Company badge (i.e. house flag) in the centre was to be of the enamel type. This is an extremely rare example of a shipping line stipulating the means of manufacture of badges for a particular class of employee. All other badges were embroidered, and that is the form that has been reproduced here. The Orient Line Petty Officers badge, with the blue wreath, was worn by both male and female employees, although blue wreaths and lace were otherwise characteristic of members of the Women's Royal Naval Service. Women officers serving in the Orient Line wore a badge with a black wreath.

A NOTE ON ILLUSTRATIONS

All the cap badges shown here have had to be drawn especially for this study. There are many reasons for this. Backgrounds used in display cases or storage cabinets are variable in colour and texture and ambient lighting gives an inconsistent result when objects are photographed. Some objects had to be photographed behind glass which invariably produced a cast or reflection that obscured part of the image. The condition of the badges that were examined varied enormously. While it is remarkable that many examples have survived at all and that individuals or organisations have seen fit to collect them, they have nearly all been worn in a hostile environment. Some have been attacked by moths or other insects, for example. Others are now extensively corroded, which is hardly surprising given the likelihood of contact with salt water. Others are discoloured or have bits missing. For all these reasons it was found early on in the project that drawing each badge was the only way to provide consistency and allow comparisons to be made. This also means that some badges and other items of dress could be reconstructed, sometimes from fragmentary evidence. For example, the Shaw, Savill and Albion cap badge (no. 256) has had the anchor added in the illustration as while the specimen that was examined did not have one, photographs would strongly suggest that one should be included.

The example for which the evidence is most fragmentary is the cap badge of the Great Eastern Railway (no. 119), the search for which in some ways started the whole project. This reconstruction is based almost entirely on the historical precedent of other ship-owning railway companies combined with an indistinct photographic image. At best it has to be said that the suggested reconstruction is plausible, for at the present time nobody seems to know exactly what this badge looked like. It is to be hoped that a specimen will eventually come to light.

For some reason, railway companies, while meticulous about marking their property and recording every detail of their livery, stopped short of any mention of their shipping interests. A good example would be the North Eastern Railway which was granted powers to own and operate ships in August 1905, and which owned docks at Hartlepool, Middlesbrough and Hull as well as on the Tyne. The railway operated a joint company, Wilson's and North Eastern Railway Shipping Company from 1906, and took over the Hull & Netherlands Steamship Company in 1908, yet the North Eastern Railway recorded nothing about the livery of any of its ships' crews. There is a very detailed account of the dress of the company's servants, no doubt intended for prospective manufacturers, which gives detailed instructions for the making of everything from stationmasters' coats to that of its dockside workers, but that stops short of recording anything of the ships' crews, their badges or uniform.

Among the badges illustrated in this work are some for which there is no matching example in the great Hawkins collection in Merseyside Maritime Museum. This collection of nearly 600 specimens must rank as one of the most comprehensive ever put together. Even so it is still true that a number of other collections hold one or two specimens that are not represented in the Hawkins assemblage, which would suggest that there are many more examples of cap badges, perhaps from the smaller companies, to be discovered. Although manufacturers' records have not survived and are not available to check, we can see from the index numbers on surviving record cards that a large number of different designs must once have been in production. See the example on p. 26 where the manufacturer's number is 104453, for instance. An unknown percentage of the numbers would, of course, have been used to record insignia for institutions that were not necessarily connected with the sea.

While it's almost certain that every railway company with shipping interests would have had a uniform cap badge of some sort, there are other institutions that owned vessels and that, in all likelihood, also had a badge. For example, the provision of Port Health Authority uniform is mentioned in the Minutes of Southampton City Council, but no illustration, if one ever existed, has survived. The dress was said to be 'Naval style' with a white cap cover, but without reference to the badge that the Port Health Inspector for whom the uniform was supplied would have worn on his hat. It is highly likely that civic pride would have ensured that many local authorities, particularly those that were owners of vessels, would have possessed unique cap badges, even though their appearance or very existence has passed from memory in many cases.

Some people query the wisdom of the Committee of the Board of Trade involved in the creation of standard uniform in consulting shipowners across the range, from those with the largest fleets down to those with as few as three vessels. Discussions with shipowners of a more modern age have revealed the importance placed on the 'ownership' of unique insignia which is felt to validate the individual identity of the firms concerned. In one particular case, that of Solent Aggregates, the appearance of the badge was debated long and hard when the firm was established in the 1960s and the result, an unusual one, is shown as no. 259 (p. 43). It represents the company funnel, the only other known example of which is the machine-embroidered badge of Union Towing & Transport (UK) Ltd of the 1970s, a decade or so later.

Adherence to regular company-based livery tended to come with the advent of steam power which is why only those owners of mechanised fleets are tabulated here. There were however many operators of sailing vessels who, in later years, also had their own distinguishing cap badges. Hawkins has examples of a few of these as does the National Maritime Museum. Joseph Conrad was photographed with fellow crew members, all wearing company rig. An image also exists in a private collection of the master of a Liverpool-based sailing ship of the fleet of Robertson, Cruikshank & Co. While Captain Jenkins himself was not photographed in uniform, his officers and apprentices all wear the company badge on their caps.

Dr David Jenkins, a noted authority on the South Wales tramping companies, is very clear that these operators of small coastal steamships were not, by and large, organisations that cared much for the niceties of uniform, although some are still represented in the Hawkins collection. These smaller concerns, the badges of which have so far escaped academic notice, include Idwal Williams, Edward Nicholl, R. Chellew and the Pentwyn Steamship Company. If these have slipped under the radar, who knows what others remain to be discovered?

4

MEDALS, DECORATIONS AND AWARDS

Please refer to the two diagrams on pp. 46–7. In addition to the regular gear which identifies our seafarer in terms of his employer and his office on board the particular ship on which he was serving, an individual may well have been entitled to wear other insignia. He may, for example, have achieved some recognition for service if he had been involved in a particular conflict, or been decorated for valour if he had performed some act of bravery beyond the call of duty. He would therefore, in both cases, be entitled to display the appropriate ribbon or, depending on the circumstance, the medal or decoration, or a miniature version of it. With ordinary day wear it would just be the ribbons that were worn but recipients of the various decorations are furnished with clear guidance on appropriate dress for more formal occasions.

The diagrams therefore attempt to chart the dates of introduction (and demise in some cases), of the awards that our seafarer might have been eligible to wear, and to record other changes such as the introduction of a new ribbon. In real life there is an order of precedence for medal ribbons when worn, with the highest award being nearest the sternum or centre of the chest. The sequence shown here relates to the date of introduction, so the order of medals encountered in a photograph for example, would not be the same as shown here.

In the case of medals awarded by various societies relating to seafarers, the ribbon could mask details of the several grades or degrees for which a medal could be awarded. The very first awards that were available to seafarers, the RNLI Medals, came in three grades, of which the gold and silver versions were introduced in 1824. A bronze medal was introduced nearly a century later in 1917. The vast majority of these medals have been awarded to the RNLI's own personnel but all share the same ribbon, no matter whether the recipients had been awarded a gold, silver or bronze.

The medal of the Liverpool Shipwreck and Humane Society also has three 'grades', of which the gold and silver were instituted in 1840 although the first medal was not actually presented until 1844. A bronze medal was introduced in 1874. While primarily awarded for saving or attempting to save life at sea, the conditions of the award were altered during both World Wars so that they could be issued for courage in the face of enemy action. The last gold medal was awarded during the Second World War.

The Shipwrecked Fishermen and Mariners' Royal Benevolent Society was founded in 1839. The ribbon and a 'tin' version of the medal were used as a membership badge and the Society has mainly been concerned with the welfare of survivors and their dependents. Some gold and silver medals have been awarded by the Society for the saving of life at sea.

Royal Humane Society medals comprise three different ribbons. The first were the Silver medal of 1775 followed by the bronze medal of 1837. The ribbon of the silver medal was later changed as shown. A gold medal, the Stanhope medal, was added in 1873. Queen Victoria gave permission for the Society's medals to be worn on the right breast in 1869 which is why the first two appear under this date on the table.

There are three Lloyd's medals as shown. Lloyd's Medal for Saving Life at Sea was instituted 1836 and became Lloyd's Medal for Saving Life in 1974. It has been awarded in gold, silver and bronze versions although only one gold medal has ever been issued. Lloyd's Medal for Meritorious Service was instituted in 1893. Between 1893 and 1900 it was in bronze only, from 1900 to 1917 was issued only in silver and from 1917 in both silver and bronze. Lloyd's War Medal for Bravery at Sea, which was instituted in 1940, was first awarded in 1941 and was last issued in 1948.

On the left breast, the Most Excellent Order of the British Empire has five levels which are indistinguishable by the ribbon alone. The Titanic Survivors' Committee, in recognition of their gratitude, presented the officers and crew of RMS *Carpathia* with what became known as the Carpathia Medal, in one of gold, silver or bronze. In conformity with

usual practice at the time, the master and medical officer received the gold medal, the other officers the silver and the rest of the crew the medal in bronze. This award was a unique occurrence applicable only to those few individuals serving on board the *Carpathia* at the time and it is not known whether any of them actually wore it. The ribbon of the Carpathia Medal was a plain crimson.

A new introduction, instituted in 2005, is the Merchant Navy Medal which is awarded annually for meritorious service and courage afloat. Its presentation is administered by the Merchant Navy Welfare Board; current rules decree that it is to be worn on the right breast.

The Liverpool Shipwreck and Humane Society and the Royal Humane Society, recognising that they were broadly covering the same activities, have agreed to cover different territory. The LSHS now confines its attention to rescues that take place in its waters, or involving Liverpool registered ships, or to seafarers from Merseyside, Lancashire or Cheshire.

Campaign medals, of which the Transport Medal is the earliest and the Arctic Star the most recently created, are shown with the correct start date, were generally awarded some time after the event and were not presented over a prolonged period. The length of ribbon shown here is primarily to render it visible to the viewer. The *Southern Daily Echo* of 4 November 1903 reported that:

> The King received in the grounds of Buckingham Palace, this morning, about 150 officers of various ranks connected with the transport service, and conferred upon them the special transport medal awarded for services in connection with the China and South African campaigns … The recipients were made up of captains, first and second officers, engineers, pursers and doctors. Some were in uniform and others in civilian attire. They were drawn up in line on the lawn, and the Royal Marine Light Infantry supplied a guard of honour and band for the occasion …

Being printed in Southampton and thus the 'local' newspaper for some of the companies involved, particular note was made of the names of recipients who worked for the Union-Castle company, but it was also observed that large numbers of troops were carried on that company's regular sailings and as the vessels were not hired as troop ships, the crews were ineligible for the medal.

During the early part of the First World War the Royal Navy awards were initially not available to members of the Merchant Service. In appropriate circumstances a suitable recipient might be given a rank, possibly even posthumously, in the Royal Navy Reserve in order for an award to be made. Towards the end of the war, lower level awards were made directly to Merchant seafarers, although this was contrary to the warrant appertaining to the award. This is why the table shows the ribbon of the Distinguished Service Cross appearing during the First World War and reappearing in 1931 when MN personnel were officially recognised as eligible recipients. Members of the Merchant Navy had been eligible to receive the Victoria Cross only since their capacity for bravery on active service was recognised by an Order in Council in 1920.

The Conspicuous Gallantry Medal, Distinguished Service Medal and Distinguished Service Order were added to the list of awards for which merchant seamen were eligible in 1942 and 1943 as shown. There was a rationalisation of RN Gallantry awards in 1993 so that the Distinguished Service Medal was eliminated and replaced by the Distinguished Service Cross, and the Conspicuous Gallantry Medal and the Distinguished Service Order (for gallantry) were eliminated and replaced by the newly created Conspicuous Gallantry Cross. Unfortunately, perhaps because of the lack of consultation, Merchant Navy personnel are not yet recognised as eligible for this new award.

The Empire Gallantry Medal was replaced by the George Cross in 1940 and all living recipients of the Empire Gallantry Medal were required to exchange them for the George Cross, an unprecedented circumstance. Likewise the Albert Medal was replaced by the George Cross in 1971 and living holders were in this instance encouraged to exchange theirs for the George Cross.

The first medal ribbon and therefore the earliest appearing on the left breast, is that of the Board of Trade Sea Gallantry Medal of 1856. In principle, this is still currently available as an award, but it seems to be moribund. A medal or decoration requires the recognition of the State before it can be worn on the left breast. Many Merchant seafarers have had their deeds recognised by other countries and have benefited accordingly by receiving some appropriate token. It would be inappropriate to incorporate these in the table, but some examples of their rich diversity can be recorded here. During the First World War employees of the Royal Mail Steam Packet Company received one *Légion d'honneur*, one Croix de Guerre, one Order of the Crown of Italy, one Order of St Ann and one Order of St Nicholas. Employees of Elder Dempster added to this tally: one Serbian Order of the White Eagle and one Knight Officer of the Liberian Humane Order of African Redemption. Captain Charles Fryatt of the Great Eastern Railway was made a Knight of the Order of Leopold, posthumously and during the Second World War employees of Alfred Holt won five Netherlands Bronze Crosses and eight Netherlands Crosses of Merit.

5

DISTINCTION LACE AND

THE FOUNDATIONS OF UNIFORM

The early beginnings of a distinctive dress on board ship have been examined and recorded in the *Oxford Dictionary of Ships and the Sea*. The origins of uniform as worn at sea arose from the need, felt by officers of the Royal Navy, to distinguish themselves from the Army and also to afford sufficient distinction between their own gradations of rank.

In 1748 Lord Anson's Board of Admiralty introduced regulations to overcome 'the inconvenience arising from the want of an establishment of rank and precedence between His Majesty's Sea and Land Officers, as well as from the want of a due distinction among the Sea Officers themselves'. The need for other ranks to be identified, apart from the wearing of gear deemed at the time to be fitting for sailors, did not arise immediately. Officers did however come to appreciate the need for order and uniformity among their own men. This in turn led to considerable differences appearing between the crews of individual ships and as crew members often changed ship this could involve the individual in considerable and unnecessary expense. A standardised uniform for other ranks was therefore introduced in the Royal Navy in 1857. Approved woven designs of badges for the various grades of seamen below officer rank were introduced in 1879.

There do not seem to be any equivalent mentions of dress relating to the crews of merchant vessels. The one exception is a collection of papers collected by John Bell, a Land Surveyor and that are held in Tyne & Wear Museums' Library. These papers were issued in relation to the *Keelmen of the River Tyne* and their disputes with local coal owners. While there are several examples in this compendium of agreements commencing in the eighteenth century, the 'Memorandum of agreement between the owners of Ouston Colliery and the several persons whose marks appear below', and entered into for one year from 1819, is the first to contain the following paragraph: 'The said Keelmen are to furnish and supply their own respective, necessary and proper Working Geer [*sic*].' These documents follow a standard formula, but this new paragraph appears to be the first to include this subject which in the context, may well refer to clothing. Unfortunately the document does not indicate what the Keelman's 'geer' was to consist of, so it does not advance our knowledge except insofar that some recognition was being given to the need for standardised equipment of some kind.

Perhaps we should examine the use and meaning of the word 'uniform' at this stage. The servants of civilian organisations often wear the livery of their employers as an identifying mark. Strictly speaking, these are not uniforms unless they have been officially sanctioned by the Crown. The postal worker wears a uniform, but the railway employee, from the very earliest days of the railway network, has worn a livery. Although every attempt has been made to maintain this distinction, in everyday speech the term 'uniform' is more widely used and understood to refer to corporate identity. As an example, the concept of a standardised police uniform dates effectively from the foundation of the Horse Patrol in London in 1805, though there is some link to the earlier Bow Street Runners. We have already seen that the newly formed railway companies were keen to place their identity upon everything from pen nibs to locomotives and their employees were no exception to this rule. This not only marked the individual as an employee of the company, with consequent advantages in terms of ease of recognition, but might also foster a corporate spirit among the staff.

As this practice of identifying the servants of any given organisation was widely established by the first quarter of the nineteenth century, one must consider how it spread to the Merchant Service in something like the form we know today. The East India Company, a corporate body in which the government had no shares, received its first charter in 1600 and, as well as having trading ships, established its own private army and navy to defend and exploit its interests. By 1773 it had taken on the administration of India and had its own livery for officers. Their day dress seems to have been single-breasted and their dress attire had elaborate twists round button holes which were numerous on collars, cuffs and breasts. It therefore diverged in many respects from the Royal Navy, though officers did wear swords. The East India Company's contribution to the development of a uniform for merchant seamen was, in fact, only the introduction of the practice of wearing rows of straight lace on the sleeves of some of its 'naval' officers by the beginning of the nineteenth century.

A much more likely source of inspiration for the development of merchant seamen's uniform was that used by the Royal Navy. The operation of long-distance mail routes from about 1840 was in the hands of private steamship owners who contracted to provide the vessels and crew to carry the mail on behalf of the government. The mail was housed on board ship in special accommodation where it was guarded by a government representative in the form of a naval officer, possibly retired or on half pay. These men wore Royal Navy uniform but were fed and accommodated by the shipping company and were able to direct the master as to when he should sail or what he should do under adverse circumstances. Arrayed in their finery, such persons caused a degree of resentment on board, but also gave rise to a wish for a similarly impressive uniform. As P&O were twice censured for causing their officers to wear a rig which was thought to be too close to that of the Royal Navy, a degree of differentiation was necessary too. Of course, a number of Commanders, which was the name given by P&O to its masters, had Royal Naval backgrounds in any case and perhaps felt more confident in command when impressively uniformed. It appears that about 36 per cent of P&O masters were ex-Royal Navy at the time, with almost all the remainder being reservists. It's very likely, therefore, that an attachment to a uniform worn earlier in the careers of these men was a contributing factor in the choice of dress and their ready adoption of it.

It has also been said that the use of livery first arose in the Merchant Service among the companies that were better off and better organised.

Among these were, of course, the mail carriers as they were heavily subsidised by the government to fulfil their contracts. In *Southampton: Gateway to the World*, it is recorded that the Union Steamship Company was paid £30,000 per year to provide one sailing per month in each direction between Southampton and Cape Town. The company would not have made anything like this amount had it carried only passengers and freight, so for example when the *Dane* inaugurated the Southampton–Cape Town service in 1857 she had only six passengers aboard.

Advertisements from specialist tailors going back to 1850 specifically describe themselves as 'Mail Service Regulations outfitters' and that 'Officers of the Royal Mail Packet Companies … [would be] equipped at the shortest notice.' We must therefore look to the mail companies as the principal source for our seafarers' dress. Many other shipowners soon followed their example, including the owners of sailing ships. Once the fashion for wearing livery had become established it became possible to distinguish the various ranks and professions of men who wore this form of dress. Several key forms of distinction lace evolved among the mail companies from quite early on. The Royal Mail Steam Packet Company and the Pacific Steam Navigation Company (and later others such as Orient Line and Houlder Brothers) all used chevrons in gold on the cuffs to denote their deck officers. These chevrons all had the apex pointing up and the angle of all was 120 degrees except Royal Mail, which was 90 degrees. Surgeons on board Atlantic Transport Co. vessels in the 1890s also appear to have worn two chevrons of this type on the sleeve. The original source of the chevrons used in this way is unknown, for although believed by some to derive from the practice of the Royal Navy, a brief examination will reveal that this is not so. A more likely belief expressed in oral testimony was that this use of chevrons had some Scottish connection. This is quite likely, as the founder of the Royal Mail Steam Packet Company, James MacQueen, hailed from north of the border and would have seen marks of this type appearing on the sleeves or cuffs of members of Scottish regiments.

Chevrons were one of the earliest forms of distinction lace. The daguerreotype photograph on p. 45 of a member of the Woolcott family is worthy of study. It shows either Commander John Henry Woolcott or his brother Captain Philip Matthews Woolcott. Both became the masters of steamships, the former being employed by the Pacific Steam Navigation Company and the latter by the Royal Mail Steam Packet Company. At this distance in time nobody now knows which was which and thus the illustration could depict either. In some ways it does not matter because both companies used chevrons on the sleeve to denote rank at this early period, predating lace rank markings on the sleeve in the Royal Navy. Although the image is undated, the style of the case in which the daguerreotype is held was popular only from about 1850 to 1852 and of course other cheaper, simpler and more effective methods of making images, such as the albumen print, were fast-evolving, meaning that the daguerreotype was soon to be superseded. This photograph was certainly taken just at the time modern uniforms appeared. White trousers fell out of favour for home service with the Royal Navy in 1856.

Many companies used straight lace on the sleeves to denote rank, with Cunard being a prime example for the use of gold lace in this way. Other companies included the London & South Western Railway, the New Zealand Shipping Company, the Federal Steam Navigation Co. (from the 1920s) and the British India, Aberdeen & Commonwealth and Union Line prior to its amalgamation with the Castle Line in 1900. Other companies used the Executive curl for their deck officers, following the example of the Executive Branch of the Royal Navy of 1856. Early examples of this include such a diverse group as the Federal Steam Navigation Company, White Star, British & Commonwealth, Dundee, Perth & London Shipping Co., the Liverpool & North Wales Steamship Co., the British Tanker Company, Ben Line and Trinder Anderson. Railway companies also used this form of lace, including the Great Eastern Railway – although their lace appeared only on the right sleeve – the Caledonian Steam Packet Company and the Glasgow & South Western Railway. The Clan Line company livery approached so near to the practice of the Royal Navy at the time that it was affectionately known as the 'Scottish Navy'. Of the uniformed employees of Elder Dempster Line, only the master had a curl on his sleeve lace.

An examination of the drawings of distinction lace shows that only the top row of lace, closest to the elbow, has the curl or loop and that this faces in a direction that might best be described as turning anticlockwise when viewed from the left. The right sleeve has the direction of the curl reversed. It has been suggested that some companies, in order to promote difference between themselves and others, deliberately reversed the conventional direction of the curl on the sleeves and the Glasgow & South Western Railway seems to have been one of these.

An intermediate form between straight lace and that with a curl on the top row is lace used straight with a diamond of lace above or just intersecting the top straight row. The Royal Fleet Auxiliary sleeve lace was in this form, as was that of the South African Railways, the British

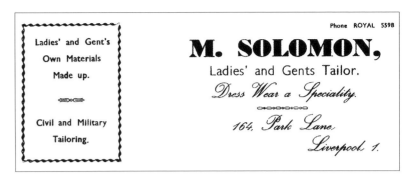

Although undated, this advertisement appeared in 1945.

Antarctic Survey, P&O Ferries (although much later), and most recently on the shoulder straps of Cunard deck officers. It actually takes its origin from a design used by the naval forces of the State of Victoria in Australia in the 1880s, and was adopted by the Australian Navy in 1903.

A few, most notably Post Office Cable Ships of the 1880s, had a wavy form of gold lace not unlike that used by the Royal Navy Volunteer Reserve, but with a wider lace and the rows closer together, and surmounted by a diamond for its deck officers (see illustration on p. 65). Then there is the standard lace which was evolved in 1919 by a government committee attached to the Board of Trade in order to form a distinguishing system for officers of the Merchant Service. Here at least one row of lace for all certificated officers or their equivalent (medical officers, for example) has a diamond in it. In the case of the master or chief engineer, where there are four rows of lace, the central two cross over twice with the upper one inverted to form a diamond. As with the Executive curl form of lace described above, this crossing over to form the diamond has a direction (see drawing on p. 50). Again there is a precedent for this form of lace.

There is a close resemblance between standard lace and that used by the Canadian Pacific Steamship Company from its foundation in 1891, although the two systems are not identical as will be seen by comparing the illustrations on pp. 50, 54. Why the government wished this pattern to be adopted one cannot be sure, but a correspondent with the *NUMAST Telegraph* stated that one Henry Moore of the Canadian Pacific Company was on the original committee that devised standard lace although this has so far been impossible to verify. Moore was certainly not a member of the 1917 Board of Trade Committee. One can only speculate that in order to be acceptable the 'standard' lace had to be different from that used by most companies then in existence and that it had to be easy to make. A variation of the design used by Canadian Pacific obviously fitted the bill. Whatever the foundation of the standard lace, its use did catch on and one finds it used by James Fisher & Sons, F.T. Everard & Sons, Risdon Beazley Ltd, Harrison's (London) Ltd, King Line, World-Wide Shipping Group, the Southern Railway and the Dundee, Perth & London Shipping Co. In other words, one can see that some of the companies, or their immediate predecessors, mentioned as having used other patterns of lace had been won over and adopted the newly created standard.

P&O had a unique system of shoulder tabs arising after their squabble with the Admiralty over the similarity of the company livery with Royal Navy uniform. An early version of shoulder tab from the 1890 book of regulations is shown on p. 49 and the later form on p. 60. This was essentially a gold strap across the shoulder that, with the creation of further lesser grades beneath the highest ranking employees, was cut into smaller subdivisions so that the tab resembled a series of square gold dots running across the shoulder.

The Royal Navy Reserve uses gold cord rather than lace. In this case two interlaced gold cords in a wave pattern denote rank, the top row of which is surmounted by a loop of two interlaced gold cords (see p. 65). The Marconi Company used the same cord, but without the loop, for its radio operators. An alternative to lace was to use gilt buttons, usually in threes, either on their own, as with P&O Commanders in the 1860s, or with lace as in the earliest Royal Mail Steam Packet Company. The Pacific Steam Navigation Company and Union Line used buttons and lace, as did the Glasgow & South Western Railway although in this case the buttons were applied in a vertical line. A combination of buttons with a twist of Russian braid was worn by P&O Surgeons and by members of Hull Trinity House.

The distinction lace of Stena Sealink deck officers in the 1980s and 1990s shows that creativity and diversity in the use of lacing continues into more recent times, for their shoulder straps, instead of having a curl on the top row, have an open, rather heart-shaped wave that mirrored the symbol on the funnels (see badge no. 250, p. 42).

The standard uniform regulations made it clear that a person was to wear the appropriate lace for their current function on board ship even if that person was in possession of a certificate that would enable them to hold a higher rank. It is obvious that, for example, there could be only one Chief Officer and that to have others wearing the same badges of rank would only cause confusion. Most shipping companies adhered strictly to this principle, although the British India Line evolved a very neat way of adhering to convention, but of recognising that some of their officers were more highly qualified than their post would suggest. The company had some intermediate patterns of lace for those who possessed what it termed 'superior certificates', but this practice does not seem to have been widely adopted by other companies (see p. 56).

The patterns of lace described above have all appeared in gold. Several of the lace designs can also be found in black mohair or black satin. At the beginning of the twentieth century, White Star used black mohair lace in conjunction with its day uniforms and gold on dress uniforms. Other companies used black with tropical uniforms, while others were exclusively black like Brocklebank and Atlantic Transport Line and yet others had mixed black or gold lace depending on the rank of the person concerned.

While Brocklebank and Atlantic Transport Line both used a curl in black lace, the Royal Mail Steam Packet Company used black lace chevrons on the sleeves of both surgeons and pursers in 1860. Both these ranks on P&O vessels had black velvet cuffs with gilt buttons and a twist of gold cord. Folklore tells us that black lace was adopted after 1901 as a mark of respect to record the passing of Queen Victoria, but although it is possible that some companies did change the colour of their lace as a mark of respect, the examples given above show that black lace was in use many years before Victoria's death and so was not introduced exclusively for this purpose.

Other companies used mixed gold and black lace into the 1920s, amongst whom were the New Zealand Shipping Co. and the Federal Steam Navigation Co. In both cases the Commander and Chief Officer had three rows of straight gold lace. With the former it was half an inch or approximately 12mm wide and with the latter, a quarter inch or approximately 6mm wide. The Chief Engineer, however, had four rows of straight black mohair lace. Lace could also be silver, used for example on the livery of a Steward on a cargo vessel where the company used standard lace, or for all grades of Steward from the Chief Steward downwards on Orient Line vessels.

Charles Dickens records in *Oliver Twist* that:

There are some promotions in life, which, independent of the more substantial rewards they offer, acquire peculiar value and dignity from the coats and waistcoats connected with them. A field-marshal has his uniform; a bishop his silk apron; a councillor his silk gown; a beadle his cocked hat. Strip the bishop of his apron, or the beadle of his cocked hat and lace; what are they? Men. Mere men. Dignity, and holiness too, sometimes, are more questions of coat and waistcoat than some people imagine.

However true this statement may have been in relation to civil society in the nineteenth century, it is not a fair view in the context of life at sea. Seafarers, at all levels, are ambassadors for their country as they make their way round the globe and their appearance as well as their demeanour is important, both in terms of the good name of the shipping line concerned and for the standing of the nation from which the line originates. The master of a merchant ship does not have the back up of the Naval Discipline Act to maintain order and has to rely on his personality to get what he wants. Breaches of the code of discipline can result in the seaman being 'logged', that is the recording of an offence in the ship's official record, perhaps with a fine of some portion of wages imposed, but the master has few other sanctions.

In contemporary civilian fashion, the top hat, which had first made its appearance towards the end of the eighteenth century, had replaced the cocked hat for formal wear by about 1840. This change in the style of headgear was also applied to 'dress' uniform on board the merchant fleet. A similar change took place in relation to 'undress' uniform after about 1820 following the adoption of the cap, first for informal civilian wear and later at sea. Top hats with straight sides and very high crowns were sometimes known as stovepipe hats or, in Scottish dialect, a 'lum' hat. These were worn, with frock coats, by the masters of inshore passenger vessels from the Clyde to the Thames from the 1840s. As early as 1837 it was recorded, in relation to the London and Westminster Boat Company, that 'The skipper, wearing a top hat, stood on the bridge ...'

When the Court of Directors of the Royal Mail Steam Packet Company came to consider and approve a proposed uniform in July 1841, they made no distinction between 'dress' and 'undress' uniform, but stipulated that the Captain was to wear a double-breasted frock coat, made of blue cloth, with a plain roll collar. Headgear was to be a 'black round hat or blue cloth cap'. The 'round hat' was in fact the stovepipe hat; the cap was to have a 1½in (38mm) wide gold lace band round it.

Incidentally, a double-breasted blue cloth jacket with a plain roll collar could be worn on board ship in place of the frock coat. The blue cloth cap soon became universal headwear, even for ratings, in the larger shipping companies, although ratings' caps were made without a peak. Initially, the crown of the cap was small, not very much larger than the hat band, and made without stiffening so the cap was soft. When fitted with a double cord chin strap, it was common practice either to pass one length of cord round the top and one round the bottom of the cap badge in order to frame it, or to pass the chin strap over the crown, distorting the shape of the cap. The ⅜in (9.53 mm) black patent leather chin strap as used by the Royal Navy was widely but not universally adopted by the merchant fleet.

The diameter of the crown of the cap increased with the passage of time. RN Regulations changed to a larger diameter cap in 1924. This was probably, once again, a reflection of the change in civilian fashions, certainly in relation to company livery. A letter sent in 1909 from George Greenslade, the Manager of the South Hants Water Company, to the Directors, asked if a few shillings more could be spent on a larger type of cap for its Inspectors. The water company purchased what it called 'suits' and badged caps for its Inspectors from either J. Baker & Co. or Miller & Sons in Southampton, depending on which outfitter put in the lower tender in any particular year. In the year in question, Mr Greenslade justified his request for a larger cap to be issued by suggesting that it would add to the dignity of the post and make the wearers look more important. Apart from suggesting that 'the customary (Water Company) yachting cap looks rather small', he further supported his argument by stating that 'the tramway and the police have adopted larger caps' (the Southampton Police, where the company was based, did not use helmets at this time). Once adopted by one organisation, the impetus to increase the size of uniform caps in line with changes in fashion became unstoppable.

There are examples of lace patterns for Commodores to be found here under British & Commonwealth and P&O dress regulations on pp. 63–4. The peaks of their caps had double rows of leaves numbering twenty-one laurel leaves in the case of British and Commonwealth, and fourteen oak leaves in the case of P&O. The holder of this rank therefore wore gear similar to that of a Flag Officer in the Royal Navy. On the other hand, the Chief Engineer on passenger ships of the Royal Mail Line wore six gold oak leaves on the peak of his cap and between the two World Wars the Chief Steward on Cunard vessels wore eight black oak leaves on the peak of his cap (see illustrations on p. 52).

We have seen a small but significant change in what might be termed the modernisation of uniform that occurred at the end of the nineteenth and beginning of the twentieth centuries. There was some modification to the cut of jackets for day dress and often a reduction in the number of buttons on double-breasted day dress to eight, but the changes mainly centred on the growth in the diameter of the crown of caps. We can see this growth by comparing the Uniform Regulations for Officers of the Fleet produced by the Admiralty in 1891 with the equivalent document published by HM Stationery Officer in 1937.

The 1891 Regulations stipulate that the cap is to be of:

Blue cloth with three blue cloth welts, 3¼ in [83mm] in total depth. Diameter across the top 8¼ in [210mm] for a cap of 21¾ in [552mm] circumference. Sides to be made of four pieces and to be 1½ in [38mm] deep between welts. Black mohair braid band 1½ in [38mm] wide placed between the two lower welts, joint to be in front, covered by the badge. Upper edge of braid to be left unsewn to admit bottom edge of white cover. Set on band of stiff leather or other material 1¾ in deep [44mm]. Cover white ribbed marcella.

By 1937 the regulations had changed so that the cap comprised:

Blue cloth with peak and chin strap. Crown to be circular with a diameter from 9 13/16 in [250mm] to 11 5/16 in [287mm] for hat sizes between 6 3/8 to 7 3/8. To have piping round the edge of the crown, another between the bend and the quartering and another near the bottom of the band. To have a mohair band 1 3/4in [44mm] wide with join in front covered by the badge. The band of the cap to be supported with double stiffening hessian 2 3/8 in [60mm] wide. The crown to be extended with a whalebone grommet joined with brass ferrule. Steel cap stretchers are prohibited. Chin strap of black patent calf leather, 3/8 in [9.5mm] wide buttoned with two flexible buttons placed immediately behind the corners of the peak. Peak to droop at approximately 45 degrees. White Cap similar to the blue except, crown and quarterings to be made of white horsehair and no piping round the edge of the crown. Cap Cover of white ribbed pique.

While the whole construction method has been quoted, the significant factor is that the diameter for equivalent cap sizes had grown by 1½in (38mm). A means of stiffening the crown had also been introduced to the regulations, although the Navy frowned upon the use of steel for this purpose, no doubt because of the risk of corrosion and consequent staining in a salt water environment.

Those companies that used rank distinction lace on cap bands, either a varying width of gold lace or a varying number of rings of narrow gold lace, also moved these markings to the sleeve if they had not already done so (see illustrations on pp. 64, 69). The peaks of masters' caps had often been adorned with ruched black ribbon (e.g. see the London & South Western Railway example on p. 64). At the same time, masters acquired distinctive gold adornments to the peaks of their caps to maintain differentiation and there was a trend towards the most senior personnel wearing four rows of lace rather than three in whatever pattern stipulated by the company dress regulations. This was not a question of vanity, for with the growth in the size of vessels there was a need for larger crews including a greater number of officers and therefore a greater number of distinctions of rank were required.

By the period covered by the records referred to here, a whole new category of crew, the engineers, were being employed on board ships at sea. In sailing ships, the only officers in charge had been those concerned with navigation and no other role for the officer classes was necessary. With the advent of mechanical propulsion, a whole new type of person was needed to maintain and operate the machinery that drove the ship. Perhaps because they were treated with some disdain in the Royal Navy, engineering officers and manual operatives with experience of working steam-powered machines were hard to recruit at first although the task might have been made harder simply because it had never been done before. The more senior recruits were, initially, drawn from either the railways or the shipbuilding companies as both concerns employed men with relevant experience. In terms of the impact on dress, the early means of distinguishing this class of crew can be seen in the distinction lace illustrated on pp. 48–9 depicting the Royal Mail Steam Packet Company and P&O. In fact the Engineers' Department reached its peak, in terms of number, in the days of steamships. The passing of steam propulsion has had a further impact on the modern insignia for ratings which has no need for a badge for the fireman or trimmer, for example. Note that the badges prescribed by the standard uniform regulations, use the Royal Navy term of 'stoker' instead of 'fireman' – the man who tends the fire (see p. 67).

The system of colour identification for occupation was first introduced in the Royal Navy in 1863 and those companies in the Merchant Service that used colour in this way adhered more or less to the RN system. P&O was unique in using blue cloth as the background for the shoulder straps (P&O Binders as they were called by Gieves) of their deck officers until he advent of new cap badges and a whole new system of rank designation in 1972.

Otherwise various shades of blue cloth have been used for Ticket Agents on Canadian Pacific, Nursing staff on British India, and the Cruise Director and Hostesses on Royal Mail Line and British & Commonwealth Line spanning a period from at least 1930 to 1970 (see illustrations on pp. 55, 57, 62). British & Commonwealth Line also used blue cloth to distinguish Refrigeration Engineers (p. 61).

Pursers had existed from early times and originally were in charge of handling money and keeping accounts on board ship. In modern times, and especially on board passenger or cruise ships, the Purser has come to be part of a separate department with Stewards, especially on the larger vessels. Since 1980, the post of chief steward on Cunard vessels has been termed the 'Hotel Manager' who runs the 'hotel department' in charge of all aspects of passenger comfort on board. Pursers, and later Hotel Managers, have worn white cloth with lace since the introduction of standard lace in 1919. Incidentally, research in the archives of tailors and ships' outfitters suggests that members of the hotel department on board ship spend by far the most on livery, no matter the size of the organisation for which they work. Perhaps this is an indication of the pride in personal appearance necessary for a seafarer in this role?

Green was not one of the original colours chosen to distinguish branches of the Royal Navy. Dark green was used for insignia to identify those employed in the Electrical Branch from 1918 and emerald green was used from 1923 for the Special Branch of the Royal Navy Volunteer Reserve. In the Merchant Service we find dark green used as the background colour to distinction lace worn by Electrical Engineers in companies such as British & Commonwealth. Other companies such as Union-Castle, Royal Mail Line, Orient Line and British India Line gave its Electrical Engineers a vivid grass green. Grass green was also frequently associated with Radio Officers where companies employed their own personnel and so a need arose, for example, on board ships of the British & Commonwealth Line, for two shades of green to be used for insignia in order to distinguish the Electrical Engineers from the Radio Officers.

Wireless Operators, as they were originally known, were a new introduction to the ranks and occupations that worked on board ship early in the twentieth century. The first British ship to be equipped with the new Marconi apparatus was the *Lake Champlain* of Beaver Line in May 1901, followed a month later by Cunard's *Lucania*. The very first two ships to be equipped in 1900 were respectively German and Belgian. Of British ships, there were sixteen vessels fitted with radio by 1903 and thirty-eight by 1906. Such was the benefit of this system that by June 1913 there were 686 vessels able to communicate in this way, although not all of these were British of course. In 1907 the Anglo-American Oil Co. fitted a system for radio communication to two tankers, making them the first non-passenger merchant ships to carry the apparatus.

Merchant navy clothing ration book of the Second World War era. Rationing of clothing continued until March 1949. This book uses the same points system as operated for civilian clothing. It is worth nothing that the seafarer still had to relinquish.

The need for an ability to communicate over long distances became obvious during the First World War and in July 1916 it became mandatory for all Merchant ships over 3,000 tons, whether passenger or not, to carry radio. This requirement was extended to ships over 1,600 tons in 1917. As a consequence of this technological change, the importance of the Wireless Operator on board ship grew enormously. Marconi, the pioneering firm, trained 3,300 men for this role during the First World War and supplied personnel to many of the major shipping companies. These men were therefore in, but not part of, the crew and wore a separate uniform. The original cap badge is no. 174 on p. 37 and the lace, which is rather like that worn by officers of the Royal Naval Reserve but without the loop, is shown on p. 65.

Ultimately Marconi was not the only provider of personnel and equipment that the shipowner could use. Other companies in the field were the Radio Communication Company, Siemens and Lodge-Muirhead, together with other foreign companies like Telefunken. Some companies employed their own staff in this field and several varieties of lace are shown in the illustrations, many of which employ the vivid green mentioned above. The introduction of standard lace in 1919 brought in a new pattern of gold lace for Wireless Operators in the form of a wave (see p. 50). Marconi adopted this lace as well as the Merchant Navy standard cap badge. The amplitude of the wave of the lace is not specified and could vary considerably, with the result that one can look at a photograph of Wireless Operators, not only from the same company, but on board the same ship and see a range of sizes of wave. All that *The Tailor and Cutter* tells us is that for a Third Wireless Operator the first crest of a wave is 2½in (64mm) from the edge of the sleeve and the lace is ⅜in (9.5mm) wide. For a First Wireless Operator the diamond between two rows of wavy lace is of ¼in (6mm) gold Russian braid, 1½in (38mm) across the points with the centre being 2¾in (70mm) from the end of the sleeve. Black braid was used as an alternative to gold.

The term Wireless Operator was changed to Radio Officer in 1937 as a consequence of the efforts of the trade body, the Association of Wireless and Cable Telegraphists, which then became the Radio Officers' Union. This organisation also lobbied to have the wavy lace of the standard uniform brought in line with the pattern used for designating other officers as they then were, and for the use of green cloth as a background. It won its argument with the Board of Trade and the appropriate Order in Council was made to change the regulations only in 1967 (see illustration on p. 65). Marconi had by this time been training suitable employees as Radio and Electronic Officers in order to keep pace with developments in shipping, and these individuals could then be seconded to large fleet operators such as Shell. Modern communications have progressed to the extent that specialists in radio communication are no longer necessary on board ship. By about 1995, Cunard had retrained its remaining Radio Officers to maintain its gaming machines although personnel from Marconi continued to be employed on ships until the late 1990s.

Colours to distinguish a person's role on board as described above were abandoned by the Royal Navy in 1955, but not by the Merchant Marine where they are still used, where applicable, today. In spite of the loss of the Radio Officer and some posts in the Engineers' Department that are now obsolete, the diversity of ranks and designations continues as requirements change. It is not many years since Trinity House offered sponsored cadetships for the new breed of Electrotechnical Officer necessary to maintain increasingly complex systems on board. In addition, the 1980 regulations of the Cunard Steamship Co. (p. 64) list the modern phenomenon of a high-ranking Security Officer, a post which has replaced that of Master at Arms, essentially a ship's policeman. So as crime, or the potential for it, goes high-tech, so in fact does the operation of a ship.

DISTINCTION LACE

The Royal Navy adopted stripes on the sleeve as the principal means of distinguishing rank only in 1856. David Gieve recorded this moment as the point of creation of the modern naval uniform. However, we learn from company regulation books that distinction lace was worn on the sleeves of companies such as the Royal Mail Steam Packet Company and the Pacific Steam Navigation Company from the early 1850s.

The lace of the Royal Navy was initially ⅝in (15.88mm) wide and the first Merchant lace was ⅜in (9.53mm). Later, many merchant shipping companies increased the width of their lace to ½in (12.7mm), a size that was later adopted for standard lace from 1919, together with ¼in (6.35mm) wide lace for some lesser ranks. At the same time, the width of lace used by the Royal Navy was reduced to ½in (12.7mm). In other words, for a short time, the lace used by the Royal Navy and the Merchant fleet were the same width. However, the width of standard lace was reduced during the Second World War to ⅜in (9.53mm), that of the Royal Navy having already been increased in 1931 to 9/16in (14.29mm). Many companies that used their own patterns of lace, continued to adhere to ½in (12.7mm) wide lace, or reverted to it in the post-war era in combination with ¼in (6.35mm) for lesser ranks. British India and Royal Mail at this time had three gradations of width of lace, with a ⅜in (9.53mm) in between.

The lace need not necessarily have been in gold. New Zealand Steam Ship Co., Federal and the White Star Line for example, all used black lace at one time. Where gold lace was used, an assay standard was stipulated by the Royal Navy of 2.5 per cent gold. This percentage of gold used in the lace was reduced as an economy measure at about the time of the Second World War. After the war, Gieves claims to have been the only manufacturer to adhere to the pre-war standard and used silk thread of a distinctive and unique colour that made the finished lace appear brighter and more vivid.

Although company regulations were explicit in giving the dimensions of the lace required, that used on the garments could actually differ from the standards laid down. Customers seeking uniform lace from some suppliers in standard form or for Royal Mail Line or Shaw Savill for example, and that was supposed to be ½in (12.7mm) wide, were being supplied lace that was ¹⁵⁄₃₂in (11.9mm) or even ⁷⁄₁₆in (11.11mm) wide. The wearers of the finished uniforms may have been quite oblivious to this discrepancy at the time, even in proximity to their colleagues wearing regulation lace. This is very probably a demonstration that one gets what one pays for, but it was certainly one way of effecting an economy in the production of uniforms.

Staff from every specialist tailor in a particular port would regularly visit the local docks and go on board merchant ships, whether the vessels were regular visitors of not, in order to renew contacts, discharge existing orders or solicit new ones. These salesmen often visited at random times after reporting to the master, and effectively started on the bridge of the ship and worked their way down, via the radio operators.

Prospective customers were visited both in their 'offices' or places of work, and in their cabins. The exceptions to this were the engineering officers who, owing to the nature of their work, generally had to be seen between 12 noon and 2 p.m. when they came off duty and changed. Representatives had to be attuned to the sensibilities of seafarers, so that if a person declared themselves to be 'a Gieves's man' during a visit by someone from another tailoring establishment, he would not be disturbed again. New customers might be persuaded to try something modest, like paper collars, in the first instance and if they were satisfied with what they received might build up to ordering a full uniform at a later stage. Representatives visiting a ship in port could either measure crew members for bespoke garments or take orders for ready-made items. In the case of

bespoke garments, if the work room was able to progress it promptly, the item could be brought back for a trial fitting on the vessel's next return to port, with the object of having everything complete for the visit after that. Because of the regularity of passenger services in some ports, this arrangement was easier than in others where the ship might call only at irregular intervals. Even so, it was a long and tedious business compared with the very rapid turnaround that was effected by tailors working in many Asian ports.

These tailors' representatives also fulfilled other functions. Some firms employed subcontractors who could undertake dry cleaning or minor repairs, so the flow of garments might be a two-way one. So too was the flow of information that the tailors' representative could pass on. A good example of this comes from British India Line which published an official staff list only every two years. This meant that, if a colleague was promoted or left the company, retired or transferred to another vessel, the easiest way to find his current status was to ask the man from the tailors' who may only have seen him a few weeks before.

As off-the-peg garments were kept in stock sizes to expedite orders, so too were the regular forms of lace kept ready-made up for sewing to the sleeves. Only unusual items were specially ordered in from a sub contractor although Miller, Rayner and Haysom made up their own lace diamonds for 'standard' uniforms on the premises. Tailoresses in the work room would generally machine-stitch the pre-formed lace to the garment unless the customer specifically asked for it to be handsewn, as was the practice with Royal Navy lace. Applying the lace by hand incurred additional cost.

The customer also had a choice in the quality of the fabric that was used to produce their garment depending on the amount they wished to spend. All garments in the period under discussion were produced from natural fibres. Wool in the form of worsted was made up into doeskin, serge, pilot cloth or barathea. Doeskin with its lustrous finish and tight steep twill weave was the most desirable and expensive with the hopsack weave of barathea being at the other extreme of cost and appearance. The twill weave of serge, a fabric often used for military uniforms, represented an intermediate quality while pilot cloth with its thick nap and heavy weight was generally reserved for overcoats. Indigo, a plant-based dye imported from India by the East India Company, was the only navy blue dye available before the advent of synthetic dyes in the middle of the nineteenth century. A white fabric used by all ranks was plain-woven cotton duck. This same material in different grades could be used for hammocks, hatch covers, boat covers and work clothes. Cotton with a ribbed weave known as marcella or piqué was often used for white cap covers.

Shipping companies got in touch with the badge manufacturers directly if they wanted a new design, and the manufacturers were keen to compete for this business. A tailoring firm would therefore receive what was required when the manufacturer was asked for the badge for a specific company and rank and therefore the outfitters did not need, nor do they seem to have produced, their own catalogues. There does not appear even to have been a standard reference work that could be used to identify the uniform requirements for a specific shipping company.

Where the particulars were not already known, it is believed that reference would be made to the relevant company rule book. A tailor who was a specialist in the manufacture of garments for Cunard said that 'for engineers, the distinction colour for the Royal Navy was "ruby" and this was also used by Cunard. Other merchant fleets used a darker purple.' It is not known how this tradition arose as it does not seem to be recorded anywhere and it is likely that the wearers were unaware of this difference themselves. In fact, the Royal Navy regulations tell us that colours were introduced in 1863 and were originally made from 'velvet' and later 'cloth' with the colour chosen for Engineers being 'purple'. Incidentally the Civil Branch of Engineers in the Royal Navy had been instituted in 1837.

The trade publication for the garment industry, *The Tailor and Cutter Ltd*, produced a compendium of designs entitled *Uniforms for the Services*. It covered male and female garments, describing itself as a 'cutting and constructional guide for suppliers'. It is undated, but it is clear from the contents and the quality of the print and paper that it was published during the Second World War in order to assist manufacturers. The first section, although headed 'Royal Navy' actually begins with a section on 'standard' Merchant Navy lace and then goes on to reefer jackets, trousers, skirts, etc. applicable to both RN and the Merchant Service. The only design attributed in this guide to any specific firm, and indeed to a specific designer, is battle dress which was widely taken up in the Merchant Navy during the Second World War (see p. 65). The blouse for this form of uniform was created by J. Hudes of Sunderland & Sons, Glasgow.

6

SUPPLIERS OF COMPLETE GARMENTS

Tailors specialising in the supply of complete garments for the Merchant Service developed from the 1840s in line with an expansion of need. Garments were both ready-made and bespoke and by and large were assembled in the work room using ready-made components from specialist manufacturers, such as the button maker, lace maker and badge producer. In the beginning these specialist tailoring firms served local communities and, apart from seafarers, were unknown beyond their own area of the country. By amalgamation or otherwise, some of these gradually extended their operations to cover many of the country's major ports and therefore to dominate the industry.

In this context it would be useful to quote two advertisements from the 1853 Southampton Directory which support the idea of small or localised suppliers. R.D. Ellyett of 165 and 166 High Street described his business as suppliers of 'Naval and Military Uniforms, Liveries, etc.' and of being 'Mail Service Regulations outfitters, etc.', while Henry Pinhorn of 20 Bernard Street described himself as a supplier of 'Regimental and Naval Uniforms, [and] Servants' Liveries', and claimed that 'Officers of the Royal Mail Packet Companies … [would be] equipped at the shortest notice'. Henry Pinhorn had lately moved his business from 178 High Street, so was clearly established before the date of this advertisement, although he had disappeared from the directories by 1859.

Even within this specialised trade there were what might be termed sub-specialists. The Capital and Labour Clothing Association of 33 High Street, Southampton operated between about 1900 and 1918 and is known to have supplied Stewards on board ship, including a member of the crew of the *Titanic*. In Liverpool the 'complete outfitter' for Stewards and Cooks, at least according to a 1914 issue of *The Marine Caterer*, was Percy Lees of 65 County Road, Liverpool. According to a former manager of Miller, Rayner and Haysom's Southampton branch, the five main Merchant Navy outfitters in the town after the Second World War all supplied female uniform which was then mostly for Pursers, but that these garments were only available bespoke; in other words, female uniform was not available off the peg. Monnery's, the firm which gradually became the principal supplier of female uniform in the port, did not even have a work room and so this element of their work had to be subcontracted. The preferred tailor was Mr Edmunson in St Mary Street, or if he was unavailable, Mr Blackburn.

E.J. Monnery & Son Ltd were based in London, Southampton and Liverpool and were in operation at least from 1918 to the 1960s. Prior to this, female crew were principally employed as Stewardess, tending the needs of female passengers. Between the two World Wars, their uniform requirements were catered for by the Nurses' Outfitting Association Ltd of 57b Renshaw Street, Liverpool with branches at 3 Above Bar, Southampton and 179 Victoria Street, London. An advertisement of September 1923 sums up the firm's own view of its position:

> We are official outfitters to most of the great shipping lines and the manageresses at the branches below are thoroughly conversant with Stewardesses' needs and know the exact regulation styles of all the companies. All White Star requirements (women's department) are stocked and urgent special orders can be completed in a few hours.

Perhaps the most highly specialised outfitters catering for the Merchant Service were those that dedicated themselves to supplying radio telegraphists. There were two firms specialising in this field, Self & Son of 79 Fenchurch Street, London and Harvey's of 10 Hart Street, Mark Lane, London. Both later moved to be more or less beside each other in London Street and both regularly advertised in the *Year Book of Wireless Telegraphy and Telephony* as being Marconi specialists though the latter also claimed to '… hold the largest stock of white suits in London', referring presumably to tropical gear. Advertisements for both these firms appear on pp. 13–4.

Returning to general suppliers of uniform for seafarers, the principal trade directory for Liverpool was *Gore's Directory* which began publication in the eighteenth century. In contrast with Southampton, none of the Liverpool outfitters associated themselves with clothing for the Merchant Service until 1883. In that year one finds Charles Bell & Son of 30 Lord Street; Edmond M. Davies of 7 James Street; Louis Davis and Co. and John J. Rayner & Sons (Navy and civil clothier) of 51, 53 and 54 Regent Street. This group is joined the following year by T.B. Johnston (naval, military and ladies' habit maker) of 5 and 7 Lord Street. Other specialist tailors were, in Liverpool, M. Solomon (whose advertisement appears on p. 81) and in Southampton in the 1920s, S. Alterman & Son of Bernard Street who described themselves as suppliers of 'Mercantile Marine Uniforms of every description'. The Water Guard which has been variously linked with the Coastguard, Customs and Excise and, in so far as it exists at all today, with the UK Border Agency, had a sole contractor for the supply of its uniforms after the Second World War, with Wather and Gardner of Bristol. The firm of Glen & Powell was also active in London and Tilbury at this time.

Messrs Gieves Ltd the naval outfitters, entered the Merchant Navy market by opening dedicated branches in Liverpool in 1921 and Southampton in 1927 although these closed in 1966 and 1970 respectively. This search for uniform business was extended from fighting to merchant ships. The 1920s and 1930s were pre-eminently the era of the great passenger liners and the international rivalry for the Blue Riband of the Atlantic Crossing to and from New York. Uniform requirements for officers on the crack ships of the great Lines were no less demanding than for the Royal Navy itself and it was natural for Gieves to seek this additional source of business from officers, so many of whom had served in the RNR. The firm became Gieves and Hawkes Ltd in July 1975.

J. Baker & Co. Ltd were in business in Southampton in the 1920s and closed in the 1970s although they had become the principal subsidiary of Gieves after the Second World War. The connection was not mentioned to customers to preserve the superiority of Gieves, but those who were in the know purchased their uniform items from Baker's believing that they were getting a better class of product at a lesser price. There were branches of Baker's in Liverpool, Tilbury Docks, Avonmouth and the Royal Albert Docks, London (see the Baker advertisement on p. 77).

S.W. Silver & Co., later Silver & Edgington Ltd, were the oldest tailoring firm in the industry, claiming to have been established in 1795 and had premises in London, Portsmouth, Southampton, Liverpool and Falmouth. George Miller, later George Miller & Son and Miller & Sons were established in Fenchurch Street, London in 1818, and later had branches at Royal Albert Docks, London and at Tilbury Docks. The firm also had premises in Southampton from the early 1850s. George Samuel Haysom Ltd were based in Fenchurch Street, London and had a branch in Rotterdam after the First World War. By this time three of the companies mentioned above had come together to form Miller, Rayner and Haysom Ltd in September 1914, with shops in Liverpool, Southampton and London. The firm styled itself as 'Suppliers of RNR and all companies' outfits'. The firm also had a branch at the foot of Wind Street in Swansea, but neither this nor the Glasgow branch is mentioned in advertisements. Later the firm became Miller, Rayner, Danco and formed the Practical Uniform Company in conjunction with Garroulds in the late 1980s. This partnership lasted until July 2002 when the firm became Miller Rayner Ltd. It still exists as a manufacturer of uniform workwear and is based in Southampton. E.J. Monnery & Son Ltd were based in Fenchurch Street, London from 1842, with branches in Southampton and Liverpool. Originally the firm supplied canteens, sea chests and cabin furniture for emigrants, but later diversified into the production of clothing, including uniforms. Davies and Smith had premises in Bute Dock, Cardiff and at Barry. Hughes and Sterling were based in Keble Road, Bootle, Brown's in Hull and Lake & Sons in Plymouth. In fact, virtually all the UK's major ports possessed at least one specialist tailoring firm catering for the needs of seafarers and some had as many as five from which to choose. Deck crews could obtain approved uniform emblems from the Tailor's Shop in Liverpool Sailors' Home.

Nationally, Gieves and Hawkes is still the market leader in the field and the continuation of Miller Rayner has already been mentioned. Other firms that remain in this trade today include S.M. Bass & Co. (Manchester) Ltd of Cheetham Hill, Manchester and Paragon Street, Hull, where 'everything from complete uniforms with all necessary accessories and smart, hard-wearing footwear, to home water wear and tropical kit is available to suit both male and female crew members of all ranks'. The firm of Len Beck, Endyke Lane, Kingston upon Hull, which was founded in 1934 and is now one of the UK's leading suppliers, states that:

highly trained staff have years of specialist merchant navy uniform experience and you can rely on the best advice and assistance with your order. We can deliver royal & merchant navy uniforms, braids & accessories throughout the UK and abroad for all ranks – male or female.

In Scotland, Clyde Marine Uniforms can be found on Govan Road, Glasgow.

Another way of looking at the uniform question is to describe it by the modern term 'workwear'. P&O was aware of this and already owned Spring Grove Services, a well-known company in the field of workwear rental, when it established a new subsidiary Design Sense, which was based in Basingstoke. This firm was launched at the Career and Workwear Show in October 1990, and expanded the business into the design and manufacture of 'corporate wear' supplying clothing for the service industries where making a good impression was important.

The name 'workwear' conjures up different images in the mind from that of 'uniform'. Perhaps it loses some of its glamour and produces a vision of drudgery, but that need not be so. Best Marine Trading Pvt Ltd of Mumbai seem to have struck the right balance. To quote some of its literature, its 'uniforms … convincingly portray the authority of the wearer' and 'keep the cold out and the warmth and smartness in'. Being ISO certified, it was the first marine supplier in the Indian subcontinent to focus on safety and quality. In fact, an emphasis on safety is culturally acceptable today, as there is no point in having the shiniest shoes if they are slippery on deck. In some environments, visibility is an important consideration. This kind of thinking is in accord with the trend towards a relaxation of formality in the workplace.

TROPICAL UNIFORM

Tropical uniforms are often referred to as 'whites' although examination of the uniform on p. 70 will show that they are often far from white. In fact, the dress worn in the tropics was as variable as standard undress uniform. Where occasion demanded there were also white versions of company mess dress to add to the complexity.

At a time when caps generally had navy blue crowns, white covers were worn in tropical climbs in combination with the conventional reefer jacket and white trousers, often, though not always, with white boots or shoes. A typical example from the turn of the twentieth century is shown on p. 70. In the 1860s companies like P&O offered crews the option of wearing a straw hat in hot weather instead of a white cover to the ordinary cap.

A single-breasted tunic jacket with a stand collar has replaced the blue reefer jacket, at least since the First World War. Apart from company buttons, rank was shown by means of shoulder straps. P&O never used this garment, but wore a much more modern-looking and comfortable single-breasted white jacket with a roll collar in conjunction with a white shirt and black tie (see illustration on p. 51).

The formality of the tunic jacket or its equivalent was retained on passenger ships, but some companies operating transports or cargo ships offered their crews the option of wearing a short-sleeved white shirt, white shorts and white stockings while in the Tropics. These were all 'Navy pattern' and a typical example is shown on p. 70. On the same page are two variations on this theme that were used by companies to express their individuality. Some preferred a grey-blue shirt as exemplified by the uniform of the Pacific Steam Navigation Company. Note that his shirt is capable of taking distinction lace in a soft form of a sleeve over a strap which is an integral part of the shirt. Another example shows the tropical gear of Port Line that chose khaki as the colour for its tropical gear.

Headgear has already been mentioned, but some companies allowed the use of white helmets in the tropics. These were also worn with a white puggaree, a scarf or band wound round the crown of the hat and which, in some cases, could be arranged to cover the back of the neck. This practice lasted at least into the 1950s with lines such as British India and the New Zealand Steamship Company. Ratings on board ships where Navy types of blouses were worn also changed from blue to white in warmer climates.

Standard Uniform for the

Mercantile Marine

The committee established by the Board of Trade for considering and reporting on mercantile uniform, comprised twelve appointees plus the Secretary J.B. Harrold, and began work on 30 March 1917. Although this date is now taken as the starting point for the creation of standard uniform, a reader to the *NUMAST Telegraph* some years ago wrote that in 1836 a House of Commons Select Committee was appointed to investigate the causes of shipwreck and that arising from this came the idea of a standard uniform for the British Mercantile Marine. The proposal came to nothing, although in 1907 the *Nautical Magazine* again advocated a standard uniform for the Merchant Service.

The 1917 Report itself sets out the reasoning behind its existence. This was principally owing to the practice that had developed since the outbreak of war of wearing merchant livery while ashore as a way of indicating that the wearer was engaged in active service during wartime. This aroused the interest of the Admiralty, which noted that some elements of company liveries were very like naval uniform and contacted shipowners about certain features of which it did not approve. These included the use of a Tudor (i.e. naval) crown on cap badges and the use of gold foliage on the peaks of some masters' caps that was very similar to that used on naval uniform. In addition, some distinction lace was the same width as that used by the Navy and the top row of some of this lace had an executive curl, again mirroring naval practice. At this point the various officers' associations approached the Admiralty to indicate that the time was right for the creation of a standard uniform, taking the opportunity to remove or avoid the elements that had caused discontent.

There was one further reason for the proposal to establish a standard uniform as voiced by the officers. The report rather coyly states that 'certain international complications' had thrown into doubt the position of merchant seafarers, or their officers, during wartime. This is taken to refer to the incident where Captain Fryatt, master of a Great Eastern Railway steamer, was executed by the enemy, reputedly for having tried to ram one of its submarines, which as a civilian was contrary to wartime convention. Fryatt was shot at the Aurorahof in Brugge on 27 July 1916, with two spies, Abel Riviere OBE and Leopold Brion. Fryatt was posthumously made a Knight of the Order of Leopold. A standard uniform, if worn by members of the mercantile services during wartime, would have made Fryatt's position clear. Ronald Hope, who brings the most recent interpretation on this incident, points out in *A New History of British Shipping* that this was followed by the British Mercantile (Uniform) Act of 1919 which did what an Order in Council could not do and provided penalties for the misuse of the new uniform. In this respect, it conveyed the same sentiments as the Uniforms Act of 1894, which were:

1. it could not to be worn without authority except in stage representations, and
2. it could not be brought into contempt.

Incidentally, the British Mercantile (Uniform) Act was repealed on 1 January 1996 as it was superseded by some of the provisions of Merchant Shipping Act of 1995, with much the same effect.

Only eight of the committee members signed the finished report. Major Maitland Kersey and S.J. Lister didn't take part. Captain Charles H. Holttum and Captain Alfred Toms did not subscribe to recommendation 2, which was that:

Any existing shipowning company or firm shall have the option of retaining its cap-badge for the use of masters and officers whilst employed on board ship, or when engaged on the ship's business ashore, but should any officer desire to wear uniform on shore on any other than ship's business, it shall not be any other uniform than the Standard national uniform in its entirety.

After undertaking some research among shipowners and officers' organisations, the report was submitted nine months later on 14 December 1917.

Messrs Maitland Kersey and Lister of the Liverpool Steamship Owners' Association filed a minority report which was appended to the main one. This decried standard uniform indicating that:

1. it was impossible to implement during the war,
2. it would be unnecessary afterwards,
3. company livery promoted discipline, and
4. company livery made identification of the person easier under circumstances where a fear of espionage loomed large in the popular mind.

A supplementary Report on Standard Uniform for Petty Officers followed on 18 January 1918. Captain Dudley North and Captain John Grace of the original appointees did not append their names to this report for reasons that were not stated, although the other committee members did.

From this it's pretty clear that there was never wholehearted unanimity as to what should comprise standard uniform even among its proponents. A further Order in Council was made in December 1921, authorising the use of a company badge to be worn with standard uniform provided that said badge had existed before 4 September 1918 a clause that went some way to removing some of the reservations of the committee.

As a result of these deliberations, standard uniform became available and was first seen in use in 1919. As a separate though related act, King George V went on to create the Merchant Navy in 1922 in recognition of the vital contribution made by the country's seafarers during the First World War. From 1926 it became customary to confer knighthoods on selected masters of shipping companies. The king further enhanced the status of the Merchant Navy by appointing the Prince of Wales (the future

Edward VIII and later Duke of Windsor) 'Master of the Merchant Navy and Fishing Fleets' in 1928. This title is now held by Queen Elizabeth II.

Incidentally, King George V, while effectively promoting standard uniform and the Merchant Navy, also sanctioned the use of the imperial crown on the buttons of both the Royal Mail Steam Packet Company and the Pacific Steam Navigation Company in 1921. The approved design showed the crown over the company initials in a sort of palace script. Both these companies already used this crown on their respective house flags and cap badges, and early in the reign of Queen Victoria their buttons had featured the royal coat of arms.

There was one further argument in favour of standard uniform, that it assisted officers on tramp steamers who often changed company in order both to maintain employment and to advance themselves through the ranks and who would now no longer be obliged to go to the trouble and expense of purchasing new uniforms every time they moved ship. As actually introduced, standard uniform used a diamond as a signifier for surgeons and pursers, which is not what the regulations stated (see illustrations on p. 51). These men would have to have had Board of Trade certificates to pursue these professions, to qualify for the diamond according to the rules. Furthermore, illustrations show coloured cloth in the centre of the diamond which is not always encountered in reality.

The colours of fabric used to identify various departments in the Merchant Service fringe both sides of the gold lace in standard uniform, whereas in the Royal Navy the colour occurs only between the rows of lace, making a further deviation from the Senior Service. Note also that, according to the regulations, only First Radio Officers had the right to wear a diamond although all radio operators had to have a licence from the Postmaster General. Nevertheless, the introduction of this lace, while the cause of some discontent among other grades of Radio Officer, was novel as the use of radio only became mandatory during the First World War.

Furness Withy adopted standard uniform in the early 1970s because the interchange of personnel within the group, the members of which had different traditions, was causing considerable confusion and no doubt expense. So although it has been suggested that nearly half the shipping companies had adopted standard uniform by the mid-1920s – although these were only the smaller operators – further adoptions were made at different times by larger companies for practical reasons.

9

ADDITIONAL ITEMS OF DRESS

SWORDS

Stories abound among seafarers about the shipping company that sought permission from the Board of Trade for its officers to wear swords and received the reply that they could, so long as they were worn on the right and so could not be drawn by a right-handed person. The company to which this story relates changes according to the part of the country in which one lives. Both Clan Line and Ben Line have told this story about each other. A variant is that when P&O asked permission for its officers to be allowed to wear swords, the company was told that indeed they could so long as the swords were wooden.

Joking apart, there were many merchant seafarers who were Royal Naval Reservists and would have been entitled to wear swords with their dress uniform. Captain Smith of the *Titanic* was such a person and his RNR sword was presented to the Borough of Southampton by his wife and daughter following his death. The Master Mariners in Southampton have a P&O dress sword, one of very few surviving examples (the National Maritime Museum has another). The topic is briefly touched on in the history of P&O uniform by Captain Barry Thompson.

We should not forget that royalty, when addressing their Merchant fleets, have worn swords. The standard Merchant Navy sword of Edward VIII when Prince of Wales is kept by the National Maritime Museum as is the rest of his Merchant Navy uniform. One might wonder just how 'standard' this sword was. A casual reference to the wearing of swords on board merchant vessels occurs in the diary of a passenger on board the SS *Great Britain* reporting on what we today would think of as a disciplinary hearing. On 4 October 1853, Annie Hemming wrote:

The Court was held in the Smoking Room and the Captain and all the officers and midshipmen attended, in their uniforms with swords on,

which report says they did not very well know what to do with, but got them continually hitched between their legs and among the benches, thereby creating much confusion.

Captain Bernard R. Matthews was master of the SS *Great Britain* at the time and his First Officer was the genial Shetlander and Royal Naval Reservist John Gray, who succeeded Matthews on his resignation in 1854.

On another occasion on the same vessel, Captain Gray, as he had become by then, was knocked down and effectively taken prisoner when he confronted a group of intoxicated Cornish miners in the bar. These men were complaining about the standard of food provided for passengers travelling in 'steerage', the lowest class and therefore cheapest accommodation. The ringleaders were apprehended and the Captain freed only when the First Officer, accompanied by other officers, dashed in with a drawn sword. So perhaps the sword, while seldom mentioned in Merchant circles, was a necessary means of maintaining control at the time.

From about 1900, masters have been further differenced from their crews by the lace on the peak of their caps, the peak itself being covered in blue cloth rather than being patent leather. This bore an arc of leaves of either oak or laurel embroidered in gold thread. The oak leaves were affectionately known as 'scrambled eggs'. Laurel came into use with standard uniform although its use was not always adhered to, or was used by some companies in conjunction with their own company uniform, for example on the caps worn by masters in British & Commonwealth Line. If a master had been a Royal Naval Reservist, he would have been entitled to wear oak leaves on his cap in any case and generally RNR buttons as well. If laurel leaves were used, then there were eleven pairs forming the decoration, and if oak leaves were used, there were eight. As with any rule, there were exceptions of course. Canadian Pacific remained apart by employing maple leaves for its masters' caps. The Chief Engineers on passenger ships of the Royal Mail Line had a row of six gold oak leaves on the peaks of their caps, and Chief and Second Stewards on Cunard vessels had eight black oak leaves on the peaks of their caps. Where Commodores were to be found, the peaks of their caps had double rows of either laurel, as with British and Commonwealth Line, or oak leaves as with P&O.

CAPS

In the very earliest recorded instances, an alternative system of differentiating rank to sleeve markings was by means of the cap. Behind the badge was a ribbon of varying width of gold lace, or of three, two or one ribbons of narrow gold lace (or indeed none at all). Examples can be seen in the illustrations of distinction lace for the Royal Mail Steam Packet Company and the London and South Western Railway (see p. 48). This practice goes back to at least the early 1850s and is mentioned in a passenger's diary travelling on the SS *Great Britain* in 1852: 'The officers are distinguished by gold bands round their caps, & gilt buttons.' Union Line also used this system, from at least 1860.

CATS

Throughout this book it has been the human crew who have been considered. However, since ancient times cats have been carried on board ship with the intention of controlling rodents; incidentally this was the means by which domestic cats were introduced to many parts of the world. Group pictures of crews often included this important member of the team, usually in the hands of the Stewardess or Cabin Boy. There is even a photograph taken in 1922 of Captain Hailey, master of the Canadian Pacific ship *Empress of Canada*, holding his ship's cat and he obviously did not feel it beneath his dignity to do so. Since cats were ubiquitous it seems slightly odd that they did not usually carry any badge of office. However, one notable example of official recognition was 'Doodles' the official cat on board RMS *Cedric*, which was presented with a leather collar by White Star Line in 1927. This carried a brass plate with the animal's name and details including that it was born on board, together with an enamel White Star Steward's badge (as no. 294 on p. 45). Today quarantine regulations in many countries make it difficult to maintain the practice of keeping a cat on board.

BUTTONS

One of the contributing elements of a complete garment was the supply of buttons which were almost always made of pressed metal and of bright metallic appearance. Many do not have any manufacturer's name stamped on the back, but those that have been found and can therefore be proved to have been suppliers to the trade have included:

- Armfield's Birmingham
- J. Baker & Sons
- Bliss Bros Ltd
- Buttons Ltd, Birmingham
- J. & W.H. Deykin
- Firmin & Sons
- J.A. Gaunt & Co., London
- Charles Jennings & Co.
- George Kenning & Sons Ltd
- R. MacLeod
- J. Mann & Co.
- Monnery's Ltd, London
- Paisley's Ltd, Glasgow
- Stephen Simpson, Preston
- C. & J. Weldon

In later years, Firmin & Sons were the leading suppliers.

TALLIES ETC.

Ordinary and Able Seamen from larger companies were dressed in a rig very similar to their counterparts in the Royal Navy. This changed from blue to white according to the climate and in similar manner, the covers of their caps changed.

Caps also had a tally or cap band of silk, tied with a bow on the left-hand side. These were made of black silk ribbon 1¼in (31.75mm) wide and 36in (915mm) long. In the nineteenth century, tallies were often quite colourful, often having the company house flag embodied in the weave together with the name of the ship. The house flag usually flanked the name of the ship and therefore appeared twice. In the case of the White Star example illustrated here, the flags of the countries at either end of its transatlantic route were used instead.

With the Union-Castle example shown, the house flag appears only once in the centre between the two words although other ships in the fleet had two. Union-Castle was only formed in 1900 and by this time the practice of having highly decorative tallies was waning and was probably extinguished during the First World War. The practice of including the name of the ship on the tally, however, continued. The tallies were supplied by Kenning & Son Ltd in packs of twelve, for distribution from the ship's slop chest.

An interviewee who was an AB (Able Bodied Seaman, a higher rank than Ordinary Seaman) with Cunard in the 1960s told the story that some sailors used to tie their tallies in a particularly attractive 'butterfly' knot. These were much admired by passengers who often bought the whole hat as a souvenir. In order to make up for the deficiency in uniform the hats were afterwards declared by crew members to have been 'blown overboard'. It's likely therefore that there are examples of these items of apparel to be found among the effects of former passengers.

A late nineteenth-century example of the single ship name variety of tally is that which was worn on Houlder Brothers' vessel *Rippingham Grange*. A black-and-white photograph of the crew shows the lettering on the ribbon to have been shaded. The background was therefore not black as the shading was, although unfortunately the actual colour cannot be determined from the photograph because the picture was taken on orthochromatic film. This does not render colours accurately and is easy to misinterpret (for example the wrong medals have in the past been attributed to Captain Edward Smith of the *Titanic* because the colour of the medal ribbons has been wrongly represented by the orthochromatic process). The drawing in this book uses a dull red to show the contrast as the house flag of Houlder Brothers was predominantly red, but examples seen from French merchant ships have shown ribbons coloured lemon yellow, salmon pink and sky blue. At the time, other European countries tended to follow the British pattern of a black ribbon with gold lettering and accurately coloured company house flags, but it's not possible to be absolutely certain in cases where the only surviving evidence is a monochrome photograph.

When the supplementary regulations associated with standard uniform for wear by petty officers and ratings appeared in 1918, the practice of some shipping companies of weaving the relevant ship's name in their hat bands, while not insisted upon, was thoroughly recommended. A late example from the British India ship *Uganda*, dating from the 1960s, is illustrated. Union-Castle maintained the practice of using individual ship names until it ceased operations and Safmarine, the company that took over, continued the tradition with its own ship names. By this time, the general rule was for companies to have the company name alone woven on the tally and examples from Cunard and Canadian Pacific are given here. In fact, the Oceanic Steam Navigation Co. went over to having 'White Star Line' on its tallies in the 1920s and in railway fleets, the tallies worn by ratings on SR vessels seem always to have proclaimed 'Southern Railway Co.'. This may well have been an economy measure, for every ship in the fleet would once have had its own individual tally. As a final cheapening of the product, companies such as Orient Line and Bibby Line had their names printed in gold ink on ribbon which appears to be rayon or similar man-made material.

As in the Royal Navy, ranks such as Boatswain were identified by sleeve markings embroidered on a patch sewn to the uniform, either gold or red on a blue garment, or blue on a white one. Examples can be seen in a page of the 1930s Toye catalogue reproduced on p. 23. These markings

Miller, Rayner advertisement of 1967 featuring a steward in evening attire. Collars on these white jackets were often royal blue as with Canadian Pacific, in this case also having a gold maple leaf embroidered on either side. Those worn by Union-Castle stewards had lilac collars to match the colour of the ships' hulls.

Other advertising material by the company stated that while they had originally been suppliers of Merchant Navy uniform, they now also supplied airlines and corporate and government departments.

were of course included in the standard uniform regulations. At the same time that company house flags appeared on tallies, rank markings were also enlivened by the addition of company elements. Some showed the company emblem like the Cunard lion above the badge (item 12 on p. 67). Others, like Canadian Pacific, used the house flag in full colour in this position (item 13 on p. 67). Where the house flag appeared over a ship's wheel, in the case of Canadian Pacific at least, the rank of the wearer was that of Quartermaster not Boatswain. The Boatswain wore the wheel emblem alone.

The practice of embroidering the company logo or flag on garments extended to the aprons of stewardesses. See example on p. 68 where the motif appears where the straps join to the bib. While the Royal Navy introduced a system of badges to identify the various grades of rating in 1827, the men either made them themselves or bought them privately so that there was no uniformity of size or design. It was not until fifty-two years later that standardised woven designs appeared. Some shipping companies continued the parallel with the Royal Navy by having markings to denote long service and, one must assume, the good conduct of their seafarers. Orient Line crew, as an example, wore a woven strip on the front of the uniform which was silver for five to fifteen years' service and gold for twenty to forty-five years' service. These varied in length and had a wavy background with the Orient Line anchor at each end with Roman numerals superimposed in the centre, being V to XV for the silver and XX to XLV for the gold badges. This practice continued until the company was fully absorbed into P&O in 1960, although P&O had been a major shareholder in Orient Line since 1919.

In common with railway practice, shipping companies were prone to putting their mark on every conceivable item. On p. 66 examples of belts are shown. The upper one is of a type worn by ordinary and able-bodied seafarers, in this case employees of the Royal Mail Steam Packet Company, so dating it from before the creation of the Royal Mail Line in 1932. There is in fact a standard uniform version which is incorporated into the rig worn by males occupying the role of master of the Merchant Navy and Fishing Fleets. The lower example is a female crew belt of Union-Castle and made from petersham ribbon, as was worn by stewardesses or medical staff. It dates from the early twentieth century. Other companies wore similar belts. The buckle of the nurses working on Orient Line was predominantly of enamel.

JERSEYS (GUERNSEYS) AND BLOUSES

The guernsey woollen jumper of the seaman carries in many cases the name of the company employing him embroidered on the front, either applied directly onto the garment itself or embroidered onto a fabric panel. Examples of these are shown on p. 67. Many had the top line of words formed into an arc and items 18, 19 and 20 are examples of this style. Others had initials which were more cryptic. Number 16 on p. 67 relates to the Union-Castle Mail Steamship Company, while number 17 is a contraction for the Southampton, Isle of Wight and South of England Royal Mail Steam Packet Company, the longest of all shipping company names and which even as a monogram, would not fit easily. Numbers 21, 22 and 23 are examples from 1910, 1920 and 1930 respectively, with that of the Liverpool and North Wales Steamship Company being one of the most elaborate with the house flag and initial letters embroidered directly in wool. The Southern Railway example is a patch, hemmed with blue thread in the form of an arc and applied as a separate piece. In the few illustrations examined, neither the London and North Western Railway nor the Great Western Railway seems to have used this method of promoting themselves via their deck crews.

The seaman illustrated on p. 67 is wearing his 'Caledonian Steam Packet Company' guernsey under his blouse, an unconventional arrangement, but not entirely unknown. There are photographs of Lascar crew wearing guernseys under their single-breasted tunic jackets for warmth. In these more casual times, the guernsey has become standard gear for all ranks and has been fitted with cotton shoulder panels carrying a soft button-down strap onto which a band or sleeve of fabric with appropriate distinction lace may be placed. It might also carry embroidered patches on the sleeves such as that shown on p. 66.

10

Museums, Galleries and Preserved Material

The primary motivation for producing this work was the decline in the number of British shipping companies and with the passing of those involved, the consequent loss of knowledge that has ensued. This suggests that it is primarily an oral history, and in fact has proved to be generally the case. The shipping companies for the most part no longer exist and their business records, while preserved in some instances, do not go into sufficient detail to provide useful insights into the details of uniform and insignia. The process of research has proved that the relevant records of manufacturers and suppliers are likewise wanting. This leads us to consider if there are any tangible remains in public institutions or otherwise readily available for inspection.

No systematic survey has been undertaken of maritime collections in museums as it was felt that this would raise as many questions as it solved. Institutions such as the National Maritime Museum in London have numbers of cap badges (fifty-seven in this case according to its website), but some are duplicates and some are foreign. So merely listing how many badges are held would give an unintentionally distorted picture. The same goes for other costume items. An institution with a group of loose company buttons may quite rightly number these individually even if they formed sets, and this would distort any final total of objects, at least in the way in which they are being viewed here. This could equally well apply to other items of occupational costume such as socks and ties.

Discussions with senior staff in a number of our main museums suggest that here too very little is preserved to represent the industry. The National Museums of Wales has but one relevant set of industrial costume, the gear of a Welshman who became a master with Canadian Pacific. It actually includes everything from his long johns to his great coat and so in one respect it is fully comprehensive, covering as it does both mess dress and undress gear. Looking at it another way it is not at all representative of the Welsh shipping industry, or at least of the smaller companies that once operated out of South Wales ports. Very few of the Welsh tramp steamer companies centred around Cardiff had their own badges, or even bothered much about uniform it is true, but there were some, and one of the collections mentioned below has half a dozen examples.

Those bodies that have relevant occupational costume tend to focus on the garments of officers. This trend towards the preservation of what one might term higher status garments also occurs in other costume collections and is driven by what has survived to be collected with the less worn items predominating. There are some garments worn by stewards and stewardesses in museum collections in both London and Southampton. With cap badges, the collection of the Honourable Company of Master Mariners can be viewed in the Headquarters Ship *Wellington* during open days. Merseyside Maritime Museum was given the Hawkins Collection in 1998, which is perhaps the most comprehensive collection extant. Even so, while it contains nearly 600 cap badges, it has examples of most but not all of the specimens in this book as well as many that are not included here.

There are also a number of portraits in museums and galleries that depict the dress of seafarers and most being contemporary likenesses of the sitters, must be considered to be accurate representations. The collections of the National Portrait Gallery are mentioned in connection with wartime activities in Chapter 12. The Imperial War Museum too has relevant collections covering several areas of interest. It has at least one item of uniform, the reefer jacket of a First Radio Officer of the Second World War, in addition to lifesaving equipment, badges, medals and some portraits of individuals. Dundee City Museums McManus Galleries has the portrait of Captain William Speedy of the Dundee, Perth & London Shipping Co. which depicts him in company rig in later life. He retired in 1900 after having spent sixty years at sea. The portrait is of about 1890 and shows him with his distinction lace of the period on both the cap and the sleeve. Southampton City Art Gallery has the portrait of 'The Captain's Daughter' by James Tissot, painted in 1873. (Tissot also painted a picture entitled 'The Captain and the Mate' which may show the same two figures.) Tissot's father was a draper and his mother a milliner, so with this grounding in the clothing industry, his depictions of women's clothes are both sensitive and accurate. Here it is the two subordinate male figures that are of interest. The old man with the grey beard is the captain and wears a waterproof cover over his cap. No doubt this relates to a career under sail, for many of the artist's paintings involve sailing vessels and one appears in the background of this painting. The younger man with the ginger beard on the right, the one who has fallen in love with the daughter, wears a cap indicating that he holds the rank of Mate, signified by the two gold stripes on the mohair band of his cap. The painting records the practice of wearing the patent leather chin stay over the top of the crown of the cap which was possible until the growth of the cap crown prevented it. With cord types of chin straps on caps, where the cord is of two parts, it was also a fashion to 'frame' the company badge with these cords, one passing over the top of the badge and the other underneath. In cases where the cords are gold, they are particularly noticeable in photographs from the period between 1880 and 1900.

The National Maritime Museum lists over 7,000 items of uniform clothing dating from 1748, but a large proportion of this is to do with the Royal Navy. Merchant material is mostly from the twentieth century, but also includes uniforms of the Honourable East India Company and a quantity of smaller dress items including the Merchant Navy uniform of King Edward VIII with its sword. There is relatively little material in the collection relating to the life of the ordinary seafarer.

Southampton City Museums has an unrivalled collection of collar tabs relating to the role of other ranks such as 'Lift Attendant' or 'Lido Deck Steward', mostly from Cunard vessels. There are approximately thirty of these, together with some forty-five uniform items including tropical and mess dress, and both stewards' and stewardesses' garments. The companies covered by the Southampton collections include: Shaw Savill, Canadian Pacific, British India, Cunard, Royal Mail Line, Union-Castle, Elder & Fyffes and P&O Ferries. There is also a small collection of cap badges and thirty-five tallies, most of which are British.

The Scottish Maritime Museum has one relevant uniform and the Merseyside Maritime Museum claims to have only a few items of clothing relating to the Merchant marine, and these are mainly officers' and Mersey Docks and Harbour Board uniforms. They did, however, exhibit a 1960s Cunard Stewardesses' uniform at an exhibition in 2006. This museum also has the Hawkins' collection, by far the most extensive Merchant cap badge collection. The National Railway Museum also has a few items of clothing, badges and buttons relating to railway shipping.

11

The Impact of War on Dress

Human conflicts have influenced the Merchant marine at least as much as the armed services, by bringing them, however unintentionally, into contact with the enemy. The Transport Medal was instituted to reward those officers whose ships were involved in transport duties in the Boer War and in the China Campaign, although the vessels themselves were not involved in the hostilities. The initial batch of medals was presented by King George V on 4 November 1903, as mentioned elsewhere. As many involved were at sea on this particular date, the Government Transport Officer in Southampton presented the remainder of the medals when the opportunity arose.

Circumstances were much grimmer in subsequent wars when there were mines in the sea, submarines beneath it, and surface and later aerial attacks were possible. In these stringent circumstances restrictions of all sorts had to put in place. On the uniform front, this manifested itself in several ways. The First World War working undress jacket, often seen in photographs of the era, was only single-breasted to economise on cloth. On 16 October 1916, the Tilbury Dock Superintendent wrote to all P&O Commanders to say that: 'At the request of H.M. Government, an alteration is being made to the Company's Regulations as to uniforms, whereby all gold lace straps worn on the shoulder are to be ¼ in [6.3mm] width instead of ⅜in [9.5mm] as at present.' As a further economy measure, in July 1917, a black mohair band was introduced on Engineers' caps instead of the former 1¼in (32mm) gold band previously used. This had survived from the 1869 regulation book as illustrated on p. 49. Similar reductions in the size of lace were pursued in other companies too, but curiously the Royal Navy did not reduce the width of its lace from ⅝in (15.88mm) to ½in (12.7mm) until 1919.

During the Second World War an economy in lace was made by not having it encircle the sleeve, but only to cover the visible area. Incidentally this was found to be beneficial in terms of wear as the lace no longer rubbed on tables or other surfaces (see p. 65). On this page is also illustrated battle dress as an option for the reefer jacket and trousers. Battle dress, at least as an option, remained available in some companies for several years after the war ended (see Clan Line regulations which give an end date for this practice of 1954). The use of pressed metal cap badges has been noted elsewhere and some examples appear in the illustrations. In the First World War cap badges tended to be smaller and simpler (see no. 50 on p. 30) but were still sewn. For typical dress of all ranks during the Second World War, a series of paintings in the National Portrait Gallery show some of these features: these portraits comprise Captain Banning DSO, Captain Henry Jackson OBE, Radio Officer James G.M. Turner GC, and a Merchant Seaman in survival gear, painted in 1943. In the Second World War the question of Merchant seamen wearing uniform or uniform-like rig ashore was overcome by the issue of a small silver 'MN' badge to be worn on the lapel. Rationing was a way of ensuring fairness in the distribution of scarce items among the community and of allowing war work to take precedence. Rationing applied equally to Merchant seamen who had their own form of ration book for clothing shown on p. 85. This system lasted from 1941 to March 1949 and 'points' were taken from a person's ration book by the retailer, according to a recognised scale, at the time the goods were paid for. However, if the seafarer received new items of clothing free from one of the seafarers' charities, rather than buying them, he still had to hand over the requisite number of coupons, so for example, a pair of socks required two coupons and a jersey six.

During the Second World War the navy blue blouse of a seaman who was in the Royal Navy Reserve when called up would carry the appropriate rank badge (if any) shown on p. 67 on the left sleeve. The appropriate long service stripes appeared below, and the initials 'RNR' on the cuff (see item 15 on this page). On his right sleeve would appear, where appropriate, specialist Royal Navy markings relating to proficiency in gunnery or signalling, for example. These are not included here, but as many merchant ships were armed, he would carry the initials 'DEMS' standing for Defensively Equipped Merchant Ship, further down the sleeve if serving on one of these (see item 14 on p. 67). During the First World War a seaman would receive the torpedo badge shown on p. 66 to wear on his left sleeve if he had served on a vessel that had been either torpedoed or mined.

12

FEMALE CREW

According to the now disbanded Oral History Unit at Southampton City Council, stewardesses were the first female crew in the Merchant Service and appeared in about 1850 as the companions or chaperones to single ladies and children travelling on their own. The passenger shipping companies appear initially to have had only one stewardess per ship.

This view is corroborated by the records relating to RMSP *Tweed* which carried one stewardess who unfortunately was drowned when the ship ran aground in the Gulf of Mexico in 1847. In spite of this, the position of stewardess on board ship was much sought after. In the book *What Our Daughters Can Do for Themselves*, written in 1896, Mrs H. Coleman Davidson says: 'One would imagine that there were not many women who would care to occupy the post of stewardess on board an ocean liner, yet when a vacancy occurs there is never a lack of applicants.' She then goes on to point out that: 'They [the stewardesses] are for the most part the relatives of officers in the service – this is the invariable rule on the Cunard Line, to mention one in particular ...'

In line with the growth of passenger travel during the nineteenth century we find Mrs Mary Ann Rogers was Senior Stewardess in charge of a small team on board the LSWR steamer *Stella*, bound from Southampton to the Channel Islands, but which sank when it hit the Casquet rocks in fog on 30 March 1899. The 'Stella' memorial was unveiled in Southampton two years later in 1901, although curiously it is called by the name of the ship rather than the brave woman whom it commemorates. Mrs Rogers had actually been given the post of Stewardess with LSWR in lieu of compensation after her husband was drowned while working for the same company.

During the second half of the nineteenth century, there was otherwise little progress made in the employment of women at sea. As late as 1890, the *Official Handbook of Ocean Travel*, referring to the Brazil and River Plate Route of the Royal Mail Steam Packet Company, states that 'Each ship carries a Surgeon, whose services are given gratuitously to Passengers of all classes. There is also a Stewardess.' During the South African Gold Rush which started in 1886, we find the literature of the Union Line proclaiming that 'Each ship carries a qualified Medical Officer and Stewardesses experienced in waiting on Ladies' which would suggest that the numbers of females employed on board ship were beginning to increase, presumably in line with the increasing number of female passengers.

There is one crew photograph taken on board the Caledonian Steam Packet Company steamer *Marchioness of Breadalbane*, probably dating from 1890 when the ship was new, and which features two stewardesses. Curiously they do not have any semblance of uniform, but wear ordinary day dresses of the period. It is believed, from the absence of images of female crew on other Scottish railway steamer lines, that female crew were in fact a rarity north of the border. Contemporary accounts do not mention the presence of stewardesses on the North of Scotland, Orkney and Shetland Steam Packet Co. steamers sailing from Leith to Lerwick in the early 1960s although the records have not been checked to verify the position.

The mention of medical staff and stewardesses in the same text is no coincidence as nursing was seen as an acceptable occupation for women. Nursing bodies had also been agitating for the inclusion of nurses in the crew, principally to relieve the ship's surgeon in dealing with large numbers of routine complaints such as cases of seasickness. The principal objection from shipping companies seems to have been the cost of an additional salary combined with the loss of a cabin that might otherwise be used for paying passengers. Captain Barry Thompson, writing in the P&O journal *About Ourselves* in 1965, informs readers that the 'first of the ladies in P&O ships' were probably Nursing Sisters who made their appearance on board the company's ships between the two World Wars. Nurses were carried on Union Line ships, later Union-Castle Line, during the Boer War, both on board vessels requisitioned as troop ships as well as on ordinary passenger sailings although their presence was related to military activities. The Royal Mail Steam Packet Company, bowing to pressure, introduced what were called Nurse-Stewardesses in April 1902.

Captain Barry Thompson in part two of his work 'A History of P&O Uniforms' quoted above, indicates that after the Second World War the Nursing Sisters were joined by an increasing number of female officers:

> Details of uniforms for Nursing Sister, Children's Hostess and Stenographer were first given in the amended P & O Regulations only in 1953. These ranks were not new, but details of their uniforms had only previously been mentioned in Departmental Circulars and had never appeared before in the printed Regulations.
>
> Nursing Sisters and Children's Hostesses wore blue dresses with an officer's cap badge on the left breast. Stenographers wore a W.R.N.S. Officer's uniform but with P & O buttons and the company's cap badge on the tricorne hat. A single band of ⅛ in [2mm] gold braid was worn on the cuffs over white cloth to denote that they worked in the Purser's Department. Their title was changed in September 1960 to Woman Assistant Purser.

These women then displayed their rank using shoulder straps in the same way as their male counterparts: 'Social Hostesses first appeared on Pacific routes in 1958. Their day wear was a blue dress with a miniature officer's cap badge on the left breast.'

In the late 1960s and 1970s the rather derogatory term 'Purserette' was coined and used by several, mainly ferry, companies for women fulfilling the role of Assistant Purser. There are examples of cap badges and uniforms shown on pp. 42, 68. P&O brought in Hardy Amies to design a revised uniform for female Pursers as a replacement for the WRNS pattern, which in its original guise, had been in use more or less unchanged since the inception of that service in 1917. North Sea Ferries also updated their female uniforms in line with fashion (see illustration on p. 69). In this case, while designers from International Uniforms Ltd were brought in, the female staff were also consulted. The result might be viewed as an updating of the WRNS uniform rather than a radical departure from it. The dress for female Pursers in Viking Ferries was not unlike that of North Sea Ferries except that a 'pill box' hat was worn. In 1980 and in line with the more casual styles that were evolving for male uniforms, ferry companies such as Stena Line kitted out their female Pursers in plain blue skirts and white blouses from a well-known high street retailer, but with a scarf in the form of the company house flag worn round the neck. The end was looped through and spread out to show the flag, so it did not appear as flamboyant as the North Sea Ferries example shown. P&O Ferries did a similar thing with scarves depicting their house flag.

FEMALE EVENING DRESS

Female officers such as Nursing Sisters were expected to attend evening functions with the passengers alongside the other ship's officers. This mingling was no doubt a form of reassurance for the passengers though it necessitated long hours for members of the crew. Evening dress had to be worn on these occasions. An interviewee who worked for Royal Mail Line in the 1960s said that she wore a black dress 'with a bit of sparkle'. Although the pattern was unspecified, the garment had to accommodate miniature company shoulder straps held down by a small company button on the inner edge and a conventional steel pin at the other. Her miniature straps were supplied by S.W. Silver & Co. and had overall dimensions of approximately 3¼in (82mm) by 1½in (38mm). This lady's lace was gold over red when she worked for the Pacific Steam Navigation Co. and red over gold for the same rank in Royal Mail Line although she had not noticed this difference until it was pointed out to her. When Hardy Amies designed the new uniform for Women Assistant Pursers in P&O in February 1967, he also designed an evening dress for them. This was of 'orient blue shantung with a bold V neckline enhanced by wide shoulder straps and set off by brass buttons'.

The *Arcadia* had a class of female crew known as an 'Ambassadress'. The significance in relation to this study is the uniform that was worn, and particularly the cap badge. Women employed in this role wore a double-breasted navy blue blazer and a white pleated skirt. A male pattern of officer's peaked cap was worn rather than the conventional female tricorne hat. This cap carried a badge based on the company flag, but was in the form of a shield rather than the later ellipse, and was surmounted by the company rising sun symbol. It was therefore a half-way house between the old and new cap badges, combining elements of both and preceded the introduction of the 'new' cap badge by some two years. An illustration of an Ambassadress appeared in the summer 1970 edition of *About Ourselves*, the house journal of P&O.

In the mid-1920s two female crew members of White Star ships were the first in any company to obtain Board of Trade Lifeboat

Certificates. The image of one Mrs Palmer who was employed as a swimming Instructress, has been used as the basis for the drawing on p. 69, where she is wearing what is in effect the female version of an Able Seaman's uniform. Her beret has the Porter's type of White Star flag as a badge.

The principal supplier of uniform for stewardesses was in fact the Nurses' Clothing Association, a company advertisement for which appears on p. 16. Here the figure wears a version of the Sister Dora cap of white cambric. Sister Dora Pattison devised this plain practical bonnet to replace the frilly lace ones worn in the era of Florence Nightingale. Cambric is a plain linen or cotton fabric which is glazed and calendered. Generally the front edge was turned up although this feature was removed in the simplified design of 1915.

Another example is shown in the illustration on p. 68. Here the bib front of the apron carries a company emblem on both sides where the straps join. Examples of the White Star pennant and the Cunard lion have been seen and are illustrated here, but even in these companies most aprons seem to have been plain. The Sister Dora cap survived into the 1960s and would therefore also have been worn in conjunction with the adjoining stewardess dress illustrated on p. 68.

In contrast, nursing staff on board ship were generally more highly qualified and were dressed in a similar way to the Orient Line Sister on p. 68. She is wearing a linen square on her head which would have been secured by pins. The figure is also wearing a silver badge of the institution where she trained on the left breast and a petersham ribbon belt closed by a silver clasp-type of buckle, some of which had company logos. Her shoulder straps denote rank (and company too as there was a wide variation in pattern). The colour of day dress varied too. Sometimes the design was dictated by the company and sometimes not. One interviewee working for smaller lines bought her own day dresses where nothing was specified. These were obtained from Harrods and were either navy blue or white for wear in the tropics, with matching plastic buttons fastening up the front.

Today women who want to make a career in Britain's diminished Merchant Navy are free to progress in any department aboard ship, although it took until November 2013 for the first woman to become Captain of a P&O vessel. Two women had already achieved this rank in Cunard service a little earlier. These women are all employed in passenger ships. Perhaps Britain still has some way to go before women achieve full equality in comparison with our European neighbours, for at least one Swedish ore carrier had a female Chief Officer in 1978.

Non-European Crews on British Ships

At one time numerous seafarers from regions visited by British ships conducting the business of empire were employed as crew by British shipping companies. Only companies with relevant trade routes supplemented their indigenous crews by this means, but the existence of these extra hands was known to be vital to the effective running of the ships.

Rudyard Kipling, in the story of 'The Bridge Builders' that appears in the collection of short stories *The Day's Work* first published in 1898, tells of a fictional Lascar, Peroo, who was said to belong to an ethnic Hindu group, the Kharva, many of whom live in Gujarat. In the story Peroo is said to have risen to the rank of Serang while working for the British India Steam Navigation Company. Apart from giving details of the fictional character's place of origin, no further explanation of 'Lascar' and 'Serang' are offered because these terms were commonly known and understood at the time. The term 'Lascar' actually denotes a seaman coming from the South Asian coastal regions and was applied generically to a multiracial, multi-tribal group of men who were attached neither to any particular ship or company but could offer their services as free men where they could obtain the best employment. The three areas of the globe from which native people with a need for work and an aptitude for seafaring were drawn are indicated on the map (p. 72).

Comparison of Ranks

	British	Lascar
	British	Lascar
Deck	Bosun	Serang
	Bosun's Mate	Tindal
	Quartermaster	Seacunny
	Carpenter	Mistree
	Carpenter's Mate	
	(or Waterman)	Paniwallah
	Storekeeper/Lamp Trimmer	Kussab (Cassab)
		Khalassi
	Able Seaman	First Class Lascar
	Ordinary Seaman	Second Class Lascar

Engine Room	Donkeyman	Serang
		Tindal
	(or Waterman)	Paniwallah
	(sometimes Oilman)	Tehlwallah
	Fireman	Agwala
	Apprentice	Topas(s) (Sweeper in the RI Navy)
	Storekeeper	Cassab
Purser's Department	Second Steward	Butler
	(Chief Steward on some lines like BI or Strick Line)	
Catering	Cook	Bhandary

A P&O response to a query on the 'Lascar Question' from the Board of Trade in 1900 stated that '… the Company have [sic] carried mixed crews of Europeans and Indian Seamen in their ships for more than half a century, to the contentment and satisfaction of the crews …'

Some companies, mainly Blue Funnel, Ben Line and Shell, employed Chinese seamen of whom there were about 5,000 on British-registered ships at the outbreak of the Second World War. Almost one-third of the British shipping industry's labour force were non-European at the outbreak of the Second World War, an increase from the 26 per cent (or 52,445 persons) found when last accurately measured in March 1928.

Indian seamen, known by everyone (and not in any sense pejoratively) as 'Lascars', had been employed on British ships since the seventeenth century when they had been hired to replace European crewmen who had died from accident or disease during the voyage out to India. From the 1870s, Lascar crews became more and more common in ships trading to the Indian subcontinent, Burma and Malaya. By 1939 some 40,000 Lascars were employed as ratings on British ships. The engagement of Lascar crews in India was governed by the Indian Merchant Shipping Acts. For the British government the most important provisions were those requiring that crews could not legally be discharged in the UK, although the crew of a ship arriving in the UK could transfer its crew to a departing ship. This procedure had been devised to ensure that Indian seamen would not become resident in the UK. Imperial citizens who did become UK residents could ship out of the UK on UK wage rates and the whole point of employing Lascar crews was that they were paid one-quarter of the wage of European seamen.

There is a painting by W.L. Wyllie, RA for P&O and in that company's collection entitled 'Sunday Inspection on Board a P. & O. Liner'. The painting was completed in 1909 and shows a group of Lascar seamen lined up against the rail of the ship with the inspection party headed by the Commander, approaching from the right of the view. The Commander is wearing the 1869 uniform and has six pairs of buttons on his frock coat. This painting is surprisingly like the humorous drawing that appeared in *P&O Sketches* although this is of earlier date (the book of sketches appeared in about 1890). Incidentally, one of the reasons that Kipling gave for his notional Lascar leaving the service of British India Steam Navigation Co. was that he was weary of 'routine musters'.

Talbot-Booth, in one of his stirring accounts of the sea aimed at inspiring the young, uses the term 'Khalassi' which he spells 'Callassee' as a synonym for Lascar. It is a Hindi word that first appeared in English in 1800 and that while it does identify a labourer, particularly a seaman, seems to have been used chiefly to describe vernacular river boat crews where their main function was to attend to the sails and rigging. It therefore represents a sub group of Lascars who were Ordinary or Able Seamen.

Seedies and Kroomen, while both ethnically distinct, were employed by the Royal Navy from the 1820s. The RN changed the name of the relevant ratings from Seedie to Somali in 1934 to reflect their principal origin at the time. Seedies were originally considered to be from anywhere between Zanzibar and the Seychelles to Socotra, with Kroomen coming from the east coast of Africa in the area of Sierra Leone and Liberia. The Seedies were universally Muslim and the Kroomen had animist beliefs. On Elder Dempster ships, gangs of Kroomen joined ships going south at Freetown and disembarked there on the return trip having been employed mainly in painting and scraping and other general duties. Neither of these groups comprised citizens of the British Empire, and neither were Goanese Lascars, Goa having been a Portuguese colony on the Indian mainland from 1510 until annexed by India in 1961. Seedies and Kroomen in the Royal Navy signed on for three years and often settled in British territory on leaving, as the Goanese settled in Mumbai in India.

Neither Kroomen nor Seedies were grouped in a rigid hierarchical structure as were Lascars and did not have distinguishing role names. The term 'Lascar' is an ancient Persian word and was first applied to sailors in the seventeenth century. The names for the various occupations within the group, while of diverse origin, occur with minor changes and two extra terms, in the Indian Navy. The Bhandary, though, is reduced to a mere galley assistant.

Some companies who employed these crews in greater or lesser numbers are listed here. Lascars were employed by: P&O, British India, Ellerman's City Line, Anchor Line, Clan Line, Mogul Line and Strick Line. Seedies were employed by: P&O and British India. Kroomen were employed by Elder Dempster and Palm Line.

THE UNIFORMS OF NON-EUROPEAN CREWS

This is based on native costume and is intended for use in warmer climates than those encountered in Northern Europe. The terms too are native ones. It is illustrated on p. 71. The headgear for Lascars is a topi, often bound with coloured cloth to the extent that it resembles a turban. The pattern, or lack of it, signified rank on P&O vessels. On British India vessels, Serangs and Tindals wore a red twisted puggaree or light scarf round the topi, with the ends deliberately left hanging down and the Seacunnie wore the company's cap ribbon on the topi. Watkins-Thomas, writing about his experiences of Lascar crews in the P&O house journal in September 1955, tells us that the topi was most often made from canvas. At the same period, British India regulations state that the topi was to be of straw.

The body was covered by a cotton smock called a lalchi. This is normally described as being plain blue, but they seem often to have been white. Evidence for this can be found in the coloured illustrations in *P&O Pencillings* or the more cartoon-like drawings in *P&O Sketches* of 1897. British India Line defined white to be for muster clothes and blue for working clothes. Serangs or Tindals would have either elaborate embroidery on the lalchi itself or else on a separate waistcoat. The actual design would be arbitrary and variable, but generally had bands forming borders and scrolls filling in the spaces between. The pattern shown in the illustration here is derived from that used on the waistcoats of the ceremonial uniform worn by Pakistani crew on P&O passenger ships in 1992. Below the lalchi, loose-fitting white cotton ankle-length trousers were worn and a sash or belt called a rhumal was often worn over the lalchi. The rhumal had the same rank-defining significance in its fabric as did the topi. Generally no footwear was worn on deck, but the P&O uniform of 1992 incorporated sandals.

Seedies tended to be dressed in a white jubba, generally without anything round the waist, and often wore a white skull cap on P&O

vessels. British India required its 'Mohammedan Servants' to wear a black lalchi with dark blue serge trousers, a black rhumal and topi with the Company badge. These garments were to be all white for wear in the tropics, with black or white shoes being worn as appropriate. The term 'jubba' does not appear in the regulations, where it is correctly described instead as a 'robe'. It is what a Muslim would wear to prayer, especially when made in white (see illustration on p. 71).

Alternative headgear for a Serang on P&O vessels was an embroidered brimless cap in the form of a taquiyah, of dark material. These last two forms of head dress, the skull cap and the taquiyah, indicated that the wearers were of the Muslim faith. In these cases, the jubba would be restrained round the waist by a sash referred to in some companies as a cummerbund. Engine room crew wore European style boiler suits when on duty.

Goanese crew were generally Christians from the Portuguese colony of Goa and their specialised role was in effect acting as the servants of officers, or passengers where they were carried on board. They performed the role of butler or similar activities (see above), keeping themselves apart from the other Lascars. In like manner, their dress was also different. They wore single-breasted jackets with silver company buttons. On BI ships these were navy blue or white according to climate, with blue and white striped mess jackets being used as occasion demanded. On P&O vessels, this striped material was worn for everyday dress and mess jackets were plain white.

14

Cadets and Apprentices

At all levels of employment there is always a need to ensure a continual renewal of personnel in order to maintain staffing levels. At times of expansion of the industry, this rate of renewal needs to be increased. The need for a proper training programme for those desirous of going to sea was first pursued by the Marine Society in the eighteenth century (and continued in the case of this body until 1939). Other institutions followed and a big expansion in the number of training establishments took place in the middle of the nineteenth century.

As with any institutions, there was a differentiation in their roles. The four main categories that have been proposed are the public schools of the sea, giving a pre-sea education to youngsters who wished to become officers; institutions that trained their pupils to enter as ratings, although some of their number did climb the promotional ladder; those founded as industrial schools for poor boys into which category one must also include a few reformatories; and a variety of establishments which one might today call colleges. These were set up to teach more advanced theory and practice relating to the sea and to assist their students to obtain relevant certificates of competency. All of these groups fed their output into both the Merchant Service and the Royal Navy. There was also a group of highly specialised colleges, Gravesend Sea School, the Prince of Wales Sea Training School and the Limehouse establishment of the British Sailors' Society, that trained ratings and hotel staff.

Most of the above institutions used actual vessels as their premises at one time, although they were on static moorings. Some shipping companies operated what might be called school ships for their Cadets or Apprentices. These were run as commercial vessels with the difference that the majority of the crew was under training. Companies that did this were the New Zealand Shipping Company and its associate, the Federal Steam Navigation Company, British India Steam Navigation Company, Alfred Holt, Elder Dempster, Ellerman, Clan Line, South American

Saint Line, Shell Tankers and British & Commonwealth Line. The last four were engaged in this activity only briefly or in a modest way and of course their ships were all steamships. Devitt & Moore, the Union Steamship Company of New Zealand and White Star Line all used sailing ships for the same purpose in the early twentieth century. Other shipping companies took cadets in much smaller numbers on their regular sailings.

Shipping companies, from a natural tendency to protect their own interests, also supported some of the static institutions. The Bibby Line was closely associated with the Training Ship *Indefatigable*, while Devitt & Moore established the Pangbourne Nautical College although six other major shipping companies supplied members of its board, and of course there was the Reardon Smith Nautical College.

As it is the distinctive gear that they wore which interests us, cap badges illustrated in this book are from HMS *Worcester* (no. 129), HMS *Conway* (no. 128), HMS *Arethusa*, Merchant Navy College, Greenhythe (no. 176), Southampton School of Navigation, Warsash (no. 288), London Nautical College (no. 165), Wray Castle Marine Radio School (no. 230), Reardon Smith Nautical College (no. 222) and the Sail Training Association (no. 244). In addition, Pangbourne Nautical College students wore the RNR cap badge (no. 240) and the staff of TS *Mercury* wore cap badge no. 270. Badges are also known to exist for Fleetwood Nautical College, Hull Trinity Sea School, Plymouth Nautical College, Boulevard Nautical School, Hull, Watts Naval Training School and HMS *Gordon*. Tallies were worn on the caps of the boys of TS *Mercury*, Russell Coates Nautical School and the TS *Exmouth*. Incidentally the official outfitters for Pangbourne Nautical College were Messrs Gieves Ltd and to HMS *Worcester*, Silver & Co.

Post-Second World War, a common way of identifying these young people was for them to wear a small company button with a twist of Russian braid on both sides of the collar on their otherwise plain uniforms. The colour of the background cloth changed according to their department with navy blue for navigation cadets, purple for engineering cadets and white for those in the Purser's department. Examples are given in the colour illustrations for Orient Line on p. 59, and for P&O on p. 63, while the sleeve marking worn by the senior navigation cadet on British & Commonwealth ships is shown on p. 62. British India Cadets had no twist, but wore three buttons on the cuff. Standard uniform regulations stipulated two.

The term used for these young people in the standard uniform regulations is 'apprentice' and in fact the same term was used by P&O. There is no difference in the role of these recruits. The difference in designation refers to the way they were engaged by the company.

15

Shipping Companies and Badges: An Assessment

With regard to cap badges alone, in other words disregarding other elements of uniform, the reader might wonder just how many types there were. The almost complete absence of manufacturers' records frustrates any accurate survey. Some extensive collections of badges have been referred to, but even where these have been set up with a view to be as comprehensive as possible, 'new' designs come to light in a random manner. These new discoveries often pose considerable problems in identification. Unless one has some associated knowledge about its origin or there is a house flag that is recognisable, attributing a badge to a particular company is sometimes well nigh impossible. The elements that comprise a badge are selected because they are meaningful to those involved, but this meaning is often lost and unlike true heraldry, there are no heralds or pursuivants to consult.

One question that could be asked is how many badge types could there have been? Leading on from this one might wonder how many shipping companies there were that could originate designs. To get some sort of feel for this, the shipowners section of Lloyd's Register was consulted, and some basic rules were imposed to refine the search. The parameters were that shipowners recorded had to have their head office in Britain or elsewhere in the British Empire (later Commonwealth) and that they had to be the owners of steam ships or later motor ships. As has been observed earlier, owners of sailing ships often had distinctive badges too, but it was the operators of the powered mail-carrying ships under contract to the government that seemed to lead the field in the beginning, and in any case reliance on sail later dwindled to insignificance.

Owners of single vessels were removed too, partly because they were seen as insignificant and partly because others were gentlemen who owned large steam yachts which again did not conform to the standard merchant pattern. The committee established to report on the need for a standard uniform for the Merchant Service, sought the views of owners of three vessels or more. Individual vessels that were registered as companies were also removed from my search. There seems to have been some tax benefit in this exercise which has fallen in and out of favour over the years. It does not convey anything about the ultimate ownership of the vessel. Likewise, as one might expect, the operators of fishing fleets were counted by Lloyd's as shipowners, but were felt to be outside the scope of this exercise and were removed except where it was clear that a company operated other types of merchant ship as well. Finally, many merchant shipping companies have tended to be known by two names: the White Star Line was the operating name of the Oceanic Steam Navigation Co. Ltd and at the other end of the alphabet, the sole owner of the Agincourt Steamship Co. Ltd was Lloyd and Co. Examples like these were only counted once each.

The relevant shipowners in Lloyd's Register were tabulated decade by decade from 1881 to 1961. Over this period of ninety years and using the filters noted above, there were found to be 5,379 principal companies excluding subsidiaries and associated lines, from W.C. Abbott who operated the Forland Steam Boat Co. which was based in London in the second decade of the twentieth century, to the Zwicker Geldert Shipping Co. Ltd based in Lunenburg, Nova Scotia in 1930s. An interesting observation is that once established a number of companies tended to remain in existence for several decades, with many of the more prominent companies existing before the start of the survey and remaining in operation throughout the period in question. Having noted that, these companies did not all exist simultaneously of course. Only 733 were counted in 1881 rising to a peak of 1,522 in 1921 after the First World War and falling to a low of 1,186 in 1941 before rising again to 1,384 in 1961 prior to the subsequent collapse of British shipping.

Unfortunately there are many complications, which mean that the figure of 5,379 only gives a general indication as to the potential number of badge designs. The list below shows fifteen principal companies for which there is a cap badge illustration here (the badge illustration number is shown in brackets). But each one comprised a number of subsidiaries which are also tabulated. Their origins are as diverse as the companies. Some were formed by acquisitions and amalgamations while others were created with the opening of new routes. The point to note is that sometimes these subsidiaries had their own individual cap badge. Those that are known and illustrated here are marked with an asterisk:

C.T. Bowring & Co. (38)
Bear Creek Oil & Shipping Co. Ltd
New York, Newfoundland & Halifax SS Co.
English & American Shipping Co. Ltd
Red Cross Shipping Co. Ltd
Oil Tank SS Co. Ltd
Lobitos Oilfields Ltd (168)*
Bowring SS Co. Ltd

Buries Markes Ltd (58)
Canadian Shipowners Ltd
Montreal Shipping Co. Ltd
Montships Ltd
Flower Line Ltd
Jade Enterprises Ltd
Louis Drefus & Co. Ltd

Coast Lines Ltd (74)
British & Irish SP Co. Ltd (48)*
Belfast SS Co. Ltd (25)*
Burns & Laird Lines Ltd (57)*
Aberdeen SN Co. Ltd
British Channel Islands Shipping Ltd (41)*
Tyne-Tees Steam Shipping Co. Ltd
Zillah Shipping Co. Ltd
Lion Shipping Co. Ltd

Common Brothers (75)
Hindostan Steam Shipping Co. Ltd
J.P. Squance
Northumbrian Shipping Co. Ltd
Kuwait Oil Tanker Co.
Lowland Tanker Co. Ltd
Vallum Shipping Co. Ltd

Elder Dempster & Co. (96)
African SS Co.
British & African SN Co. (39)*
Elder Dempster Shipping Ltd
Beaver Line
Ocean Transport Co. Ltd
Imperial Direct West India Mail Service Co. Ltd
Elder Line Ltd
Nigerian Transport Co. Ltd
West African Lighterage & Transport Co. Ltd

Furness, Withy & Co. Ltd (109)
Hessler Shipping Co. Ltd
Gulf Line Ltd
Neptune SN Co. Ltd
W. & T.W. Pinkney
British & Argentine SN Co. Ltd
British Empire SN Co. Ltd
Empire Transport Co. Ltd
Furness-Houlder Argentine Lines Ltd
Houlder Line Ltd (139)*
London Welsh SS Co. Ltd
Temple, Thomson & Clark
Johnston Line Ltd
Johnston Warren Lines Ltd
Manchester Liners Ltd (170)*
Norfolk & North America Steam Shipping Co. Ltd
Simpson, Spence & Young
Peareth SS Co. Ltd
Beckingham & Co.
Prince Line Ltd (220)*
James Knott

Quebec SS Co. Ltd
Rio Cape Line
White Diamond SS Co. Ltd
Warren Line (Liverpool) Ltd
George Warren & Co.
Shaw Savill & Albion Co. Ltd (256)*
Warwick Tanker Co. Ltd

Hunting & Son (147)
Mineral Oils Cpn Ltd
Saxoline SS Co. Ltd
Northern Petroleum Tank SS Co. Ltd
Norwick SS Co. Ltd
Hunting SS Co. (1919) Ltd
Field Tank SS Co. Ltd
Doxfield Tankers Ltd
Eden Tankers Ltd
Ayrshire Navigation Co. Ltd
Hunting (Eden) Tankers Ltd
Northern Mercantile & Investment Cpn Ltd

Lawther, Latta & Co. (162)
Nitrate Producers SS Co. Ltd
Seafield Shipping Co. Ltd
Southern S. Shipping Co. Ltd

Walter Runciman & Co. (243)
South Shields S. Shipping Co. Ltd
Shipping & General Property Co. Ltd
Moore Line Ltd
North Moor S. Shipping Ltd
Transatlantic Carriers Ltd

Christian Salvesen & Co. (247)
South Georgia Co. Ltd
David Geddes

Polar Whaling Co. Ltd
Sevilla Whaling Co. Ltd

F.C. Strick & Co. Ltd (265)
Anglo-Algerian SS Co. (1896) Ltd
Anglo-Arabian & Persian SS Co. Ltd
La Commercialle SN Co. Ltd
London & Paris SS Co. Ltd
Strick Line Ltd, Strick Line (1923) Ltd
La Tunisienne SN Co. Ltd
Cory & Strick Steamers Ltd
Shaharistan SS Co. Ltd

Trinder Anderson & Co. (271)
Australind S. Shipping Co. Ltd (22)*
Montreal Australia New Zealand Line Ltd
Avenue Shipping Co. Ltd

United Baltic Cpn (286)
Anglo-Estonian Shipping Co. Ltd
Anglo-Latvian Shipping Co. Ltd
Anglo-Lithuanian Shipping Co. Ltd

Watts Watts & Co. (289)
Watts Shipping Co. Ltd
Eastboard Navigation Ltd
Kupan (Bahamas) Ltd
Afran (Bahamas) Ltd

Andrew Weir & Co. (9)
Ocean Nav. Co. Ltd
Bank Line Ltd (23)*
Hong Kong Navigation Co. Ltd
Indian African Line
Inver Transport & Trading Co. Ltd
Inver Tankers Ltd

In large fleets formed from existing companies with their own traditions, there was a tendency to maintain this individuality. Good examples here would be the companies forming the Coast Lines group, the badges for several of which illustrated here. The Furness Withy group also maintained this diversity until contractions in the size of the fleet and changes in the mode of operation made this difficult to maintain and a new group badge was designed by competition (no. 112). From 1919, many smaller companies used the standard cap badge and there were late adopters due to contraction and amalgamation.

Some company badges have changed for no obvious reason except for fashion. A striking example here would be the replacement of the original P&O sun and anchor with a design based on the company house flag, a change that took place in 1972 and seems to have been unconnected with any other event in the company's history. The cap badges of Coast Lines and Guinness Tankers have both changed in this way too, although only later examples are illustrated here (nos 74 and 125).

Added to this complexity, several examples of families of cap badges within a company have also been described. So, on one hand, the potential number of cap badge designs may have been reduced from our original figure of 5,379 because of the use of the standard cap badge or indeed the adoption of no livery using a badge at all. Others didn't change with amalgamation or absorption. The badge of Tyzer Line was retained when it and three other companies amalgamated to form the Commonwealth and Dominion Line. This itself was taken over by Cunard in 1916, but the badge remained the same, continuing to be used when, in 1937, the company was rebranded as Port Line (see no. 217). On the other hand, the number is no doubt increased by what one might term random changes such as those noted above, and the need in large companies to have a series of grades of identifying badge. Forgetfulness or just lack of observation seem to play a part here. A seafarer consulted for this book and who had started his maritime career working for the Crescent Shipping Company of Rochester, was adamant that the company had no cap badge although an example is shown in no. 78. The true number of badge types, while yet unknown, must run to several thousand.

EPILOGUE

As with all tales of the sea, it would be good to have a happy ending. How one views the outcome rather depends on whether one has an optimistic or pessimistic outlook. In terms of objects, little has survived, but at least some things have been preserved in our museums and other institutions to remind us of past glories. Cap badges in particular have been appreciated by private collectors for their workmanship and the knowledge they contain about our maritime history. Some of these such as the Patrick Nunney collection now with the Honourable Company of Master Mariners in London and the William Hawkins collection at Merseyside Maritime Museum, have passed to bodies where they can be consulted by the public.

The Royal Navy is often held up as the progenitor of all things sartorial to do with the sea. After all, its mode of dress was the model for almost every navy in existence. The colour system for identifying the various departments on board ship, for example, originated with the Navy. However, the Navy adopted lace for sleeve markings to distinguish rank only in 1856 and the Merchant Service can be proud to claim precedence here. Not by very much, a few years perhaps, but in this regard the merchant fleet led the way. Twice in the early 1840s P&O was effectively reprimanded by the Admiralty for wearing dress that was felt to approximate too closely to the naval pattern – it was virtually identical. This was particularly in connection with epaulettes, so the company evolved its own shoulder identification system.

The use of epaulettes with their characteristic fringe gave rise to another tale of the sea, in that the Admiralty did give permission for P&O to wear epaulettes provided they wore three. Other early mail companies such as the Royal Mail Steam Packet Company and the Pacific Steam Navigation Company led the way with sleeve lace in the form of chevrons in the early 1850s so that by about 1860, most other steamship companies then extant used sleeve distinction lace in one form or another. In fact, a board minute of the Royal Mail Steam Packet Company of 1841 proposed that deck officers should wear 'bars' of gold lace ⅜in (9.5mm) wide on the cuffs. And so this system of distinctive sleeve lace evolved with each company acting on its own for over fifty years until the Admiralty again found the practices of the Merchant Service impinging on its own. Out of this came standard uniform and the Merchant Navy. Selling the concept of standard uniform, if one looks at it in modern business terms, was not easy, and even today entirely company-based systems of crew designation remain (see examples of both Cunard on p. 64 and P&O on p. 63). Others used standard lace, but with the company badge and possibly company buttons too, as was the case with British Telecom, for example.

Dress etiquette and traditions survive on board passenger and cruise ships for those who hanker after old ways. Company livery is still to the fore here too, but not just for appearance's sake. It was always held by detractors of standard uniform that company livery established and promoted *esprit de corps* among crews and of course it has the advantage for passengers that they know who is who among the crew in order to seek advice. Company traditions are likewise associated with these distinct systems of identification. Cunard livery for example, hardly changed from that shown on p. 52 between about 1880 and 1960, except for the peak of the master's cap which originally was very similar to the P&O example on p. 49. As we live in more casual times fashions change to keep pace and we must not equate this with a slipping of standards.

There are far fewer British ships and indeed British shipping companies than formerly, so some contraction in the diversity of dress is inevitable. On the other hand, the opportunities for women to be able to follow a career at sea have increased enormously. What we should be concerned about is the decline in certain aspects of our native garment manufacturing industry, practically to the point of extinction. Is there anybody apart from the Royal School of Needlework that can actually work with traditional materials? Again perhaps this is not the way to view the problem. In a marine environment, in particular, the gold of a cap badge soon loses its lustre and cannot be revived. This is really because the wire is not pure gold by any means and soon loses its reflective surface, and so we might consider whether there are better alternatives. Computer-aided machine embroidery has entered the scene, but it does not have the bulk or reflectivity that we have grown to expect unless designs used on a badge change to eliminate foliage. The badge of Union Towing & Transport (UK) Ltd – not reproduced here – is machine-made and has no traditional 'gold' elements at all. An alternative would be to revert to one-piece metal designs, but not, one hopes, to the wartime pressed metal that tried to replicate stitched gold wire. William Scully has produced a cast bronze cap badge for the Canadian Navy which seems to have all the depth and sparkle of traditional designs and at the same time is likely to be less prone to tarnishing and this may point the way forward.

Medals and decorations also vary according to changing circumstances unlike the other areas of dress touched on here where one expects an element of constancy. The only thing that one might hope is that the current unfairnesses in the availability of awards may be eliminated so that members of the Merchant Navy might be placed on a par with the armed services.

This book is only an attempt to show the way. It is for others to pursue and to expand our knowledge of this fascinating subject.

PUBLICATIONS CONSULTED

150 Years of the Maltese Cross 1840–1990: The Story of Tyne, Blyth and Wear Tug Companies, by John H. Proud (Tyne and Wear Tugs Ltd, 1993).

All About Ships and Shipping, 6th edition, by Edwin P. Harnack (Faber and Faber, 1934).

All Hands and the Cook: The Customs and Language of the British Merchant Seaman 1875–1975, by Barry Thompson (The Bush Press, 2008).

Around the Coast and Across the Seas: Company History of James Fisher and Sons, by Nigel Watson (St Matthew's Press, 2000).

Badges and Insignia of the British Armed Services (A. & E. Black Ltd, London, 1974); section on 'The Royal Navy' written by Commander W.E. May.

Blue Star Line 1939–45, by Taprell Dorling (W. Foulsham & Co. Ltd, 1973).

Buttons: A Guide for Collectors, by Gwen Squire (Frederick Miller, London, 1972).

A Short History and Fleet List of the Canadian Pacific Ocean Steamships 1891–1956, by George Musk (World Ship Society, 1956).

Carrying British Mails Overseas, by Howard Robinson (George Allen & Unwin, 1964).

Cruise Identity, Design and Culture, by Peter Quartermaine and Bruce Peter (Laurence King, 2006).

Cunardia (The Open Agency, 2005), 'At the Helm'.

The Day's Work, 1st edition, by Rudyard Kipling (Macmillan & Co. Ltd, 1898).

The Elder Dempster Fleet in the War 1914–1918 (Elder Dempster & Co. Ltd, Liverpool, 1921).

Every Thursday at Four O'Clock, by Henry Damant (Friends of the Lion Association, 1977).

Flags at Sea, by Timothy Wilson (National Maritime Museum, Stationery Office, 1986).

Gieves and Hawkes 1785–1985, by David W. Gieve (Gieves and Hawkes Ltd, 1985).

The Gold and Silver Wyre-Drawers, by Elizabeth Glover (Phillimore, 1979).

His Majesty's Merchant Navy, 3rd edition, by E.C. Talbot-Booth, RD (Sampson Low, Muston & Co. Ltd, London, n.d. *c.* 1940).

A History of the Dundee, Perth & London Shipping Co. Ltd. and Associated Companies, by Graeme Somner (World Ship Society, 1995).

A History of the Marconi Company 1894–1965, by W.J. Baker (Methuen & Co. Ltd).

The History of the Radio Officer in the British Merchant Navy and on Deep-Sea Trawlers, by Joanna Greenlaw (Dinefwr Publishers Ltd, 2002).

Jane's Fighting Ships 1999–2000, edited by Captain Richard Sharpe, RN.

John Bell papers, Tyne and Wear Museum Library.

'Lascars in the Port of London', by J.P. Jones, in *PLA Monthly* (February 1931).

A Link of Empire (Royal Mail Steam Packet Company, 1909).

Lively Ahoy: Trinity House Pilots of the Southampton & Isle of Wight District, by George W. Bowyer (Broadbere, 1931).

Mariner's Memorabilia: A Guide to British Shipping Company China of the 19th & 20th Centuries, Vols 1 and 2, by Peter Laister (Peter & Pam Laister, 2006).

A Merchant Fleet at War 1939–1945: Alfred Holt & Co., by Captain S.W. Roskill (Collins, 1962).

The Merchant Navy, by Ronald Hope (Stanford Maritime, London, 1980).

Nautical Training Ships: An Illustrated History, by Phil Carradice (Amberley Publishing, 2009).

The Nautilus Telegraph (Nautilus International).

Navy List, January to June 1918, p. 2306.

A New History of British Shipping, by Ronald Hope (John Murray, 1990).

Northwestern Ships and Seamen, by Alan Lockett (Editorial Workshop Ltd, Preston, 1982).

Oliver Twist, by Charles Dickens (Richard Bentley, 1838), Chapter 37.

'Our Asian Crews', by M. Watkins-Thomas, in *About Ourselves*, P&O (September 1955).

The Oxford Companion to Ships and the Sea, 2nd edition, edited by I.C.B. Dear (Oxford University Press, 2005).

P&O Pencillings, by W.W. Lloyd (n.d., *c.* 1890, reprinted by P&O, 1987).

P&O Sketches in Pen and Ink, by Harry Furniss (n.d., *c.* 1897, reprinted by P&O, 1987).

Ribbons and Medals: Naval, Military, Air Force and Civil, revised edition, by Captain Taprell Dorling (George Philip & Son, London, 1957).

Royal Mail War Book, by H.W. Leslie, (Heinemann, 1920).

Royal Mail: A Centenary History of the Royal Mail Line 1839–1939, by T.A. Boshell (Trade and Travel Publications, 1939).

Rules and Regulations for the Guidance of the Officers and Men in the Service of the North Eastern Railway Company from 1 January 1920.

Sailor in Steam, by J. Murray Lindsay (Angus and Robertson, London, 1966).

Sea Hazard 1930–1945 (Houlder Bros. & Co. Ltd, *c.* 1946).

Ship Steward's Handbook, by J.J. Trayner and E.C. Plumb (National Sea Training School, Gravesend, n.d.; reprinted by Conway, 2007).

The Ship that Stood Still, by Leslie Reade, edited and updated by Edward P. de Groot (Patrick Stephens, 1993).

Ships and the Sea, edited by E.C. Talbot-Booth (Sampson Low, Muston & Co. Ltd, London, 1941).

Southampton: Gateway to the World, by Alastair Arnott (History Press, 2010).

Specifications of Uniforms Worn by Staff and Requirements Applicable to the Supply of Same, North Eastern Railway.

Standard Uniform for the Mercantile Marine.

Tracing Your Family History: Merchant Navy (Imperial War Museum, 2006).

The Trained Nurse and Hospital Review, Vol. XXXV, No. 5 (November 1903), New York.

The Training Ship 'Mercury', a History, by A.L. White (TS Mercury Old Boys' Association, n.d.).

Treatise on Practical Seamanship etc., 2nd edition (William Hutchison, 1785).

Under the Furness Flag 1891–1951, by A.J. Henderson (Furness Withy, 1952).

Uniform Regulations for Officers of the Fleet 1893 (Admiralty, London, 1893).

Uniform Regulations for Officers of the Fleet 1937 (HMSO, 1937).

Uniforms for the Services (The Tailor and Cutter Ltd, London, n.d., but Second World War era).

Union Jottings, by W.W. Lloyd (n.d., *c.* 1895).

United Towing: 1920–1990, by Alan Ford (Hutton Press, 1990).

The Victorian City: Everyday Life in Dickens' London, by Judith Flanders (Atlantic Books, 2012).

What Our Daughters Can Do for Themselves: A Handbook of Women's Employments, by Mrs H. Coleman Davidson (Smith, Elder & Co., London, 1894).

White Star Magazine.

Wireless at Sea, the First Fifty Years, by H.E. Hancock (Marconi International Marine Communication Company Ltd, 1950).

Wrens in Camera, 1st edition (Country Life).

The Year Book of Wireless Telegraphy and Telephony (Marconi Press, 1914).

The Year Book of Wireless Telegraphy and Telephony (The Wireless Press, 1918).

The Young Seaman's Manual and Rigger's Guide, 13th edition, by Captain C. Burney, RN, CB, FRGS (Kegan Paul, Trench and Trubner, London, 1901).

INDEX

Numbers of badge illustrations shown in bold.